Reference only

10. APR 97

4311   HUMPHRIS, Ted and
PALMER, Doris

DIS   D

D0298840

Northe   ies

00 300 284 311

APRICOT VILLAGE

APRICOT VILLAGE

Further reminiscences of the Aynho gardener

TED HUMPHRIS

and

Doris Palmer

DRAWINGS BY
GAVIN ROWE

PELHAM BOOKS
LONDON

Northamptonshire
Libraries

942.559
3*

00 300 284 311

Reference

First published in Great Britain by
Pelham Books Ltd
27 Wrights Lane
London W8 5TZ
1987

© 1987 by Ted Humphris and Doris Palmer

All Rights Reserved. No part of this publication may be
reproduced, stored in a retrieval system, or transmitted,
in any form or by any means, electronic, mechanical,
photocopying, recording or otherwise, without the prior
permission of the Copyright owner.

British Library Cataloguing in Publication Data

Humphris, Ted
Apricot village.
1. Aynho (Northamptonshire)—Social
life and customs
I. Title.   II. Palmer, Doris
942.5'59082'0924   DA690.A99
ISBN 0–7207–1743–4

Filmset in Great Britain by
Cambrian Typesetters, Frimley, Surrey.
Printed and bound by Billing & Sons
London and Worcester

Contents

Acknowledgements

The authors gratefully acknowledge the help and loan of photographs by Miss Gertie Garrett, Miss Nancy Stayton and Mrs Charlotte Czeppe. Our thanks to the Oxfordshire Museum Service, in particular to Sarah Gosling and Sophy Coltman and for permission to use photographs from the Packer Collection. Thanks to A.M. Cleveley of *The Field* whose article found us a publisher. Thanks to Peter Floyd for the modern photographs and to Mrs Rae Boxall for typing the manuscript. A special thanks to John Beaton of Pelham Books for his enthusiastic support and interest. Finally, and particularly thanks to Alf Palmer for his patience, forebearance and encouragement during the preparation of this book.

This book is dedicated to the past
and present residents of Aynho who
have played such a part in my life.

Also to Roisin and Russell Humphris
my great-grandchildren and to Ellen
and Ian Boxall and Ian and Timothy
Palmer the grandchildren of my
co-author in the hope that they, the
young generation, will learn to love
and cherish the countryside which is
their heritage.

Introduction

It was in July, 1981, that I first met Ted Humphris. With my husband I had moved into our retirement home in Twyford, near Banbury. During the negotiations for the purchase of our bungalow the vendor had mentioned Mr Humphris as being something of a celebrity, we were quite interested to meet him.

When we did meet we found him to be a delightful, friendly and helpful neighbour. Always ready to assist in any way possible. He steadfastly refused to give advice on matters gardening, in answer to a question he would always answer 'Well, I don't give advice but if that were mine I'd do so and so'. Just one of his funny little quirks.

One day he told me about a book he had written a number of years before, *Garden Glory*, and I borrowed his copy. It was a joy to read. Returning it I expressed the view that he should write another book. As a result of his reply he handed over to me a large pile of pieces of paper. Some typewritten, some hand written. They were on sheets of quarto, A4, the back of old calendar pages, from note books and anything else which came to hand. A glorious and frustrating collection. Frustrating because I would find so many snippets in all sorts of places. However, I realised that there was a wealth of anecdote and story which should not be allowed to remain hidden. The result follows. It is mostly in Ted's own words, except the final chapter which tells of a walk and drive I shared with Ted around his village. It was a fascinating afternoon. I found myself looking at a row of council houses but seeing small boys and girls at play in a recreation field. I looked at a beautiful and elegant home but saw a labourer's cottage, I looked at rolling fields of crops but saw a parkland with deer grazing under the trees, such was the evocative nature of the commentary by this wonderful old gentleman.

In this age of rush and bustle, of war and drugs, violence and strife, I am grateful that I have been able to glimpse, through the eyes of my friend, a way of life of which I had no real knowledge.

Doris Palmer, M.B.E., F.L.A.

Chapter One

Introduction to Aynho

The village of Aynho (previously Aynhoe) lies on the edge of the beautiful Cotswold country between Bicester and Banbury. It is on the borders of Northamptonshire and Oxfordshire, although the village is in the former county the border runs through the parkland of Aynho Park, the house which dominates the village.

Both the house and village are familiar to the many visitors and motorists who use the A41 Birmingham to London road which runs steeply through a series of bends in the village. Unlike so many country houses the house can be seen from the road. This was not always so, when I was a boy just a part of the wings and the roof were visible as there was a screen of evergreens and forest trees which were later cleared away.

The site is an ancient one. The Domesday Book referred to it as Aienho a name which means a spring or grove on a hill. The village was founded by Aega or Aegaston in Anglo-Saxon times and a descendant, Aeger who was a standard bearer to Edward the Confessor, forfeited the lands after the Norman Conquest. The lands passed to Sir Geoffrey de Mandeville, a Norman baron who probably built or enlarged an existing fortified house or castle on or very near to the site of the present house.

1

The de Mandeville family lived there for several generations and they were followed as owners, by many famous families: the Claverings, Nevilles, Fitzalans (Earls of Arundel), Shakerleys, Traceys and Marmions. In the early part of the seventeenth century it was sold to Richard Cartwright a member of the Inner Temple.

Richard Cartwright had been born in 1563, he married Mary, fourth daughter of Sir John Egerton, Cheshire. In 1615 a son, John was born who, after the death of his father, in 1637, inherited the estate.

John Cartwright was a staunch Republican and in the Civil War defended his house against the Royalist army. There was a lengthy siege but the house was finally captured by the Royalists who suffered very heavy casualties. After the Battle of Naseby where the Earl of Northampton had suffered a very heavy defeat at the hands of General Sir Thomas Fairfax, kinsman of John Cartwright, the Royalist troops retreated towards Oxford. Aynho House was set on fire, it was said that the firing was done by a member of the Earl of Northampton's family.

After the King's cause had fallen John Cartwright established a claim for £10,000 to pay for his losses but he did not live to receive this recompense for it was not finally paid until twenty years after the Restoration of the Monarchy and four years after his death.

The village could be likened to the hub in a wheel, roads radiate out of it like spokes, to Banbury, Brackley, Buckingham, Bicester and Chipping Norton. It looks out towards Banbury across the Cherwell Valley with the Oxford Canal running alongside the river and swinging round the base of the hill. Although strictly speaking not right in the Cotswolds, Aynho nevertheless looks like a typical Cotswold village with its houses built of the lovely yellowy stone. Slate or stone roofs have replaced the thatch but it still retains its charm and loving but stern control has prevented ugly urbanisation. New buildings are not too obtrusive and most follow the style of the old village.

In feudal times villagers paid to the Lord of the Manor rent for their homes and part of this rent was paid in apricot fruit, each house had an apricot tree trained against its walls. It was customary for the gardens at Aynho Park House to have a small nursery of apricot trees to replace old or damaged trees. Many houses still support their apricots so Aynho still earns its old title – the Apricot Village.

The apricot, or *Prunus armenica*, originated naturally in Armenia, Mongolia, Manchuria and Northern China. It is said to have been cultivated by the Chinese for more than four thousand years. It is claimed that the Romans and Greeks also cultivated it, as did the people of Tibet and Northern India. A Dr Bretschreider is said to have found it growing wild and in great abundance in the mountains around Peking where the fruit were red and yellow, about 1¼ inches in diameter and slightly sour but edible. This could easily be accepted as the wild progenitor of our garden apricots, these show a considerable range of varieties yet are produced from seed.

The apricot is very distinct in foliage and wood from all other species of *Prunus*, the grandular pulp of the fruit is another distinction, whilst its leaves resemble those of the Lombardy Poplar.

History tells us that the apricot was first introduced to England by a French priest who brought it from Italy and gave it to Wolff, gardener to Henry VIII in the year 1524. It has been found that the most satisfactory method of cultivation is in the form of a fan-trained tree against a south or south-west wall. The best time to plant is late October as the buds on the lower parts of the shoots mature early in the season. Later planting can be done in mild weather but never after the first week of February.

These plants were very well suited to Aynho and people took care with training and pruning. Pruning was used to restrict the tree to a desired shape as well as to enhance the quality of the fruit. Of course, there were those who pruned badly, pruning is one of the most misapplied and misunderstood arts of gardening and too often hacking and clipping are substituted for real pruning.

Pruning and training are, together, two parts of the same act because you usually lay the branch in the proper place at the time you cut it. Fan training is undoubtedly the best method of growing apricots because it obviates the risk of branches dying back which is unfortunately a habit with this fruit. All stone fruits such as peaches, plums and apricots are liable to exude resin which is gum-like in appearance and this is most likely to appear from injudicious pruning especially if a branch is cut off near the trunk in spring or summer, this should never be done as the excessive gumming which may result will, in the end, lead to the death of the tree.

Aynho soil is stoney, sandy marl with a plentiful supply of lime and this is ideal for apricots. However, the replacement trees were always bought from a North Country nurseryman, when they arrived they were planted on a south facing wall and there they grew until needed to replace an unsightly or dying village tree. The variety grown was 'Moor Park', a hardy and vigorous variety with large and juicy fruit.

Nowadays there are still many apricots on the Aynho village walls although some folk have also planted and trained other plants – there are several handsome pyracantha, wisteria and clematis montana, but Aynho will always be the 'Apricot Village'.

Chapter 2

My family and early childhood

I do not know when the tradition of planting apricot trees was first started but almost every house had such a tree trained against the wall when, in the year 1901 I was born into this Apricot Village – the village which was to be either my home or my place of work for the next sixty-seven years.

I was born on 19 November 1901, fifth child and fourth son of Joseph and Eliza Humphris, although I was the fifth child born to my parents one child, a girl, had died when an infant. My father was the son of William Humphris who lived in Kings Sutton, a village some three or four miles away and from which he had, for many years, walked to his employment in Aynho. My grandfather had been a casual worker for many years. He was well respected as a sawyer and moved around from place to place following his trade. This was a somewhat precarious way of earning a living, especially for a married man with a growing family, so, when offered a regular and permanent post on the Aynho estate he did not hesitate but accepted it and so began his daily three mile trek each way to and from Aynho. In those days working hours were long and my grandfather must have made many of his walks in darkness regardless of weather too. Perhaps he would have liked to live in Aynho but the letting of village houses was the responsibility of the estate manager, it was not a question of a worker deciding to move but of a house becoming available and the manager deciding to whom to offer it. Houses seldom became vacant though, so my grandfather walked, even as an old man (and men became old earlier in those days!) He finally was given the tenancy of one of the alms houses and from there, during the First World War, he would come out of retirement to practise another skill, that of maintaining in good order all the hand, cross-cut and circular saws used on the estate.

When my father was old enough to start work he joined his father to learn the skills of sawyer and general estate carpenter, work he continued for the Aynho estate until his retirement in 1945. He died two years later, aged seventy-three.

When my second brother, Joseph William Humphris was eight weeks old my father, mother, brother John and the new baby moved to Aynho. Until then my father had, like his father, walked the three miles each way from Kings Sutton. My family moved into a house known as number 86 but commonly referred to as 'the big house opposite the black-smiths'. Here the family settled down and grew.

As a child and young man I hardly knew my brother John for he left home whilst I was still very young, he had started work as a porter at Aynho railway station but had moved to Wolverhampton. Travel was not so common in those days so we did not see him very often but he came back to Banbury as a foreman shunter and then, for a few years before he retired he became a guard on goods trains.

Brother Joe started work in 1911 as house boy to Mr Woolnough the estate agent and then, a year later began working under Alfred Walton the highly respected estate carpenter. Eight days before his eighteenth birthday in 1915 Joe volunteered to join Kitchener's Army. He was the first man in Aynho to volunteer and, we believe, the last to be demobilised. Being under nineteen his departure for France was prevented by my mother but later he went to the trenches of the Somme. He served the rest of the war unscathed and marched into Germany, two hundred and seventy-four miles in twenty-two days and this carrying a ninety pound pack! He was demobilised and came home on Easter Sunday 1919. The train carrying him to Banbury was stopped by signals when near Aynho so he promptly jumped out, his companions threw his pack after him and he saved himself the six mile walk from Banbury.

After two weeks he returned to work on the estate, he stayed on as maintenance foreman for the new owners when part of the estate was sold in 1941 and, in 1950 he moved to a similar job at Eaton Hall, Chester, on the estate of the Duke of Westminster. He was sorely missed in the village as he had played a very prominent part in village life being secretary of the Flower Show Committee, Secretary of the Village Hall Committee, a Parish Constable and an officer in the Home Guard. With his wife, Maud, he had, for the previous twenty years, kept the village Post Office. Joe was delighted to know that this book was to be published but sadly did not live to see it as he died, aged ninety, in August 1986.

My brother, Frank, was two years older than I, also worked on the estate, first in the gardens and then as a stone mason's mate. He went into the army when he was eighteen and was wounded the first time he went into action. He came back to work on the estate until its break-up when he moved to Banbury to work for the Railway Board. He died aged fifty-one as a result of his war wounds. It took considerable effort on the part of the British Legion to obtain a war widow's pension for his wife but it was finally accepted that his early death was directly attributable to his war wounds.

When I was three months old I was ill with diphtheria, in those days a killer disease, and one from which recovery was very rare indeed. Because of this I did not later join much in the rougher games of my elder brothers and my contemporaries but spent more time with my two younger sisters, Ethel and Florrie. Ethel was two years younger than I was, although she always insisted that it was one year, eleven months and four days. Florrie was a further two years younger. I spent a great deal of time with Ethel who, although more or less a semi-invalid, nevertheless rarely complained, she had a sweet and gentle nature. I would help her with her reading and writing which may account for my love of books, a love which continues today. I cannot remember any other member of my family reading a book, except perhaps in school.

The smell of paint always made Ethel ill so when my father did any indoor painting Ethel would go to stay with my mother's friend who lived a few doors away. This was the spirit which prevailed in the village in those days, neighbours would always come forward to help in a crisis or whenever necessary. Sister Ethel was passionately fond of children and when old enough she went as a nursemaid to the children of a Banbury doctor. Against the advice of our parents and of her doctor she married and later gave birth to a little girl. She died two years later, at the age of twenty-eight in giving birth to a second child.

Florrie, my younger sister was a much stronger baby, as she grew older she would join in any game I wanted to play. In fact even today, when she is seventy-nine she is far more interested in sport than I am. Of course both sisters went to Aynho School and then, when old enough, went into service before getting married. Both dear sisters gave me a niece and they, in turn, have given me great nieces and nephews.

My father was a very good sawyer and was held in esteem by the villagers. A fine built man, he had a luxurious moustache which was the envy of many a young man and quite a source of pride to some of his mates. Indeed, a stranger once stopped at the Cartwright Arms, the 'local', and claimed to the assembled men that they had not seen the like of his moustache before, further, he declared he'd pay £5.00 to anyone they could produce who had a finer appendage. My father was fetched from home and the two moustaches carefully measured, Father's was the longest by just one quarter of an inch! So the £5.00 was duly handed over but I suspect the eventual winner was the landlord of the Cartwright Arms!

My parents never had a holiday and to my knowledge never paid a visit to any large town, except on one occasion when my father went to London. The estate manager took all the men connected with the estate to the Wembley Exhibition followed by a night at the theatre. I was the only one who did not go on this trip; someone had to stay and look after the greenhouses. I did not mind because I had already paid a visit to the Exhibition. This was when my wife-to-be and I became engaged, in the morning we went to Bond Street and bought a gold ring with a little cluster of diamonds (I paid £6.00 for it). In the afternoon we went to the Wembley Exhibition and after a high tea in Maison Lyons in Oxford Street on to the Drury Lane Theatre where, if I remember rightly, we saw *The Desert Song*. This was the first of many visits to the London ' theatres – some shows I still remember! *The Paladium Pleasures*, *The Whirl of the World*, *The Gorilla*, *The Farmer's Wife* at the Court Theatre and at the Tivoli such pictures as the *Big Parade* and *Ben Hur*. My father never spent a night in hospital and neither have I, perhaps our healthy outdoor lives prevented illness?

My mother was a careful and thrifty woman, which was just as well, my father being just the opposite. Father handed over his weekly wage and received back 2/6d (12½p), this was his pocket money from which he had to buy his own beer. Of course, in those days beer was only 1½d (about ½p) a pint so 2/6d would buy a lot of refreshment. Every night my father would fetch his drink in a milk can which held about a pint and a half. He would go across the road and up the lane called Skittle Alley to the back door of the shop which had an off-licence. Just occasionally he would have his drink in the pub but this was rare, he had to get up very early in the morning so a drink by his own fire was the norm. Father smoked a pipe and used tobacco called Shag which my mother bought for him. Each morning, beside his breakfast plate would be his daily ration of tobacco and a box of matches. I remember the matches were always Bryant and May which were bought in packets of twelve boxes which cost 3d (just over 1p). This little tradition was followed every morning, including Sundays. Father was a bellringer and helped with the hanging of the new bells when they were installed. I'm sure his pipe was never smoked in church so I expect the Sunday ration of tobacco was saved until after dinner.

My mother was a very strong character and impressed upon us children the need for thrift. She encouraged us to work and earn money which we gave to her receiving part of our earnings back as pocket money. I did not always spend mine on sweets but saved some and, when I was fourteen was the proud possessor of a Post Office Savings Book. I always tried to save a little and can remember the thrill when I drew a pound from the bank to buy for myself my first bicycle, it was second-hand but the thrill of possession was enormous. One of the creeds my mother impressed on us was 'Never buy unless you have the money to pay'. I wonder what she would think of hire purchase and credit cards? However her teaching stood me in good stead and enabled me to achieve my ambition to own my own house, what is more, I was able to pay cash for it. But that was not until 1945, a long way ahead in my story.

I now realise, with love and admiration that my mother must have led a very hard life, she must have gone without herself, possibly even knowing hunger, so that my brothers, sisters and I could always be well fed and clothed. Many of our clothes she made herself after we were in bed, stitching for hours in the light of candles or oil lamp. I remember there were clothing clubs in those days. Salesmen would call each week and offer their wares for sale. A new suit for a man would cost less than one pound, boots or shoes would be five to ten shillings a pair. For work men wore strong trousers of corduroy which, besides the usual front opening had an extra piece of material which fastened to the waistband with buttons. This was about nine inches by six inches deep and was called a 'flap-jack'.

In large families the younger children usually wore 'reach-me-downs', new clothes went to the eldest (or largest) and then down through the family. Few younger children ever had anything brand new. In the cruel way of children the wearers of these clothes were often the butt of teasing even though most were in the same situation. In some ways the girls were luckier than the boys as dresses could be altered more easily and most mothers were extremely able with scissors and needles, whilst most men repaired boots and shoes for their families.

Somehow it was considered degrading to accept gifts of second-hand clothes but no such strictures applied to buying for a penny at the jumble sale. These sales were a regular feature of the village life being organised by the Church, Mothers' Union or one of the other organisations. Indeed clothes that would be considered 'charity' if offered freely were boasted of if bought as a bargain at the jumble sale.

Like most husbands of this day, my father would retire to bed leaving my mother to clear away the supper things and prepare the table for breakfast. In those days breakfast was a very important meal especially for the working man and usually consisted of eggs, thick slices of home-cured bacon with thick slices of bread fried in the bacon fat. This meal was usually taken before 6.0 am although, if the man had a long walk to work, as did my grandfather and my father until his move to Aynho, it was more usually taken by 5.0 am, it was the only substantial meal the man would get until the evening. Another of the tasks my mother performed was to ensure that paper, wood, matches and small pieces of coal were to hand for the morning fire lighting. My father went to bed before my mother but he also got up first to light the fire to enable breakfast to be cooked as we had no gas or electric stove.

In the winter months my mother would take the live embers from the fire and put them into a warming pan which she would use to warm her nightdress and her side of the bed.

11

Most homes had a warming pan but if they didn't, bricks would be warmed in the coal oven, wrapped in flannel and placed in the bed. Some people had earthenware hot water bottles instead and if one of these developed a leak or crack it was not discarded but filled with sand, then, each night it would go into the oven to warm.

Our neighbour, Mrs Pike, had a warming pan, much to the annoyance of Mr Pike who always declared that one day she would burn him with it. Getting a little fed up with his moans Mrs Pike decided to teach him a lesson. One cold night she put the warming pan outside until it was icy, then, in her usual fashion she put it in the bed. As soon as her husband started his usual tirade she deliberately pushed the pan against his leg, his yell could be heard all down the street, but it was the end of his complaining!

There were many diversions to prevent monotony in the village life. There were regular visits by the tinker who mended kettles and pans or ground knives and scissors, and many a housewife looked for his coming when a saucepan sprung a leak or the scissors did not cut cleanly. The pedlar also did his rounds, he sold small items of haberdashery, socks and stockings, handkerchiefs and ties, it was amazing the amount he managed to squeeze into his pack. The hurdy-gurdy man was a great joy to the children, sometimes he had a monkey with him and once, to great amazement he had a dancing bear! As a child I was subject to the habit of sleep walking. I must have been so excited to see a real live bear that during the night my mother, hearing one of the stairs creak, got up and saw me opening the door. Realizing what had happened, because this was not the first time I had walked in my sleep, mother pulled a coat over her night clothes and followed me. I went to the green where the bear had been dancing, and, after standing still for a few minutes, I turned around and went back to bed still asleep. Of course I knew nothing of this till told by my mother some years later by which time I had grown out of the habit of sleep walking.

These travellers were a great asset to the village and gave

considerable pleasure by their visits. The tinker always arrived in a covered wagon and while he was busy putting a new bottom in a saucepan or making a new lid for a kettle he would regale us children with many a blood curdling tale. The pedlar was always on foot, his pack was a wicker basket, round the sides and in the lid were little pockets for small items, the needles and thread, pins and elastic. His heavier wares were arranged on the bottom of the basket – knives, scissors, boot polish or brushes. I remember the basket had sturdy little legs which kept the bottom of the basket from touching the ground. If the wind and rain were blowing in his face Pedling Jack would carry his basket on his chest, if they were blowing on his back the basket was carried behind him, this way his legs got protection as he had a waterproof cape which covered both man and basket. Sometimes he used the basket for a seat and, in wet weather when wearing his cape he was in a little tent with just his head sticking through, on this he wore a bowler hat. It was after one of his visits that the garden boy whose home was nearly a mile from the gardens and who cycled to and from work was late getting back from his dinner break. When I inquired the reason he said he saw the pedlar coming down the road and dare not pass because on the pedlar's previous visit as he rode past he had toppled the pedlar's hat off on the muddy road – he feared stern retribution!

The arrival of the hurdy-gurdy man was a very welcome event, we loved to see the little monkey which rode on his master's shoulder or on the barrel organ. The children danced to the music and their singing would be joined by the chatter of the monkey who seemed to enjoy the fun as much as we did.

Once we had a travelling theatrical company come to the village and I saw my first 'professional play', it was *Maria Marten, the Murder in the Red Barn*. Of course we had plays in the village school, put on by the village people but this was *REAL* actors and actresses, oh the glamour!

Every year there was a wood sale, the buyers came from far and wide but especially from High Wycombe for special wood for their famous furniture industry. These buyers would seek the advice of the woodmen, the 'inside' knowledge being much appreciated and usually rewarded by a liberal measure of whisky or rum. The day following the wood sale was usually one of heavy heads and hang-overs. Sometimes there were very amusing incidents, I remember a very tall woodman who had a very small wife. One day, following the annual sale the man arrived at work with a black eye. On being pressed to explain how he got this 'adornment' he told his workmates that he had needed to 'spend a penny' in the night and had, in his inebriated state, pulled from under the bed not the usual jerry but a basket of washing which his wife had washed and ironed the night before. His watering of this was not appreciated and the black eye was the result. He glanced up at the sky as he told this story and, with a deep sigh remarked 'Thank God it's a fine drying day!'

The horse drawn carrier cart made the journey to and from Banbury every Thursday and Saturday, the days of Banbury markets. The carrier did many a small errand for the village people. In my young days the carrier was Joe Bates from the neighbouring village of Souldern. He had a wooden leg but was most active getting in and out of the cart without difficulty. He had a very jolly and cheerful personality and his twice weekly visits were welcomed. Joe Bates would carry anything large or small and would search all over Banbury for something asked for by a villager. His charge was usually 2d a package. The Banbury traders used to send their errand boys from one carrier to another with packages to be delivered in the various villages.

These diversions helped relieve the arduous and hard life of the villagers. Keeping a family well fed was always a problem and I suspect that many a woman ate less than her fair share to keep her husband fit. Days off sick were days when money was lost although Aynho people were luckier than most as the Squire and his family always tried to care for their people. Indeed I remember one occasion when my mother was taken ill. We returned from school to find Mrs Cartwright, wife of the Rector, preparing our midday meal. When we had enjoyed this she told me to go that evening to the kitchen of the Big House were a meal would be waiting for all the family. My brother and I went that evening with some trepidation, we had been told to ask for the housekeeper, Mrs Day whom we thought of as being a very stern and upright lady who ruled the house with a rod of iron. Even when I started to work in the gardens I was a little afraid of Mrs Day but there was really no need to be, under that somewhat stern exterior she was a very kind and thoughtful lady. So, on this day we asked for Mrs Day and received a cooked dinner sufficient for all the family, we scuttled home with it thankfully. A meal was waiting for us every evening until my mother was well again. We always looked a little askance at Mrs Day's two dachshund dogs which were rather addicted to ankle nipping.

One must remember that in those early days of the twentieth century there was no such thing as supplementary or unemployment benefits. In Aynho help was always freely given to employees and other villagers alike, both the Park House and the Rectory were sources of help, but unless their plight was desperate the majority of the poorer people were too proud to ask for help. However, many a hint was dropped by friends and help usually forthcoming, for the very needy there was 5/- (25p) a week 'Parish Relief' but this was not much on which to feed a family and many would have gone hungry but for the help which was quickly and readily forthcoming, often this came from the wife of the Rector. Mrs W.D. Cartwright was a wife of the best type, always ready with help and sympathy when need arose.

In my childhood most people kept a pig or two and pig-meat was a staple of our diet. Cheap food was not necessarily inferior food and a sheep's head would often provide a good meal for three or four people. The brains would feed one, the tongue another whilst the rest of the head would be stewed and made into broth or allowed to set as brawn. A cow's or bullock's heart was often stuffed and roasted to provide a really

15

good meal for a family and breast of mutton made a tasty dish. In the winter there were suet puddings. Sometimes these were savoury and sometimes sweet. The savoury ones were used as a main meal. The paste would be rolled out and spread with a layer of chopped bacon, onions, potatoes and seasoning before being rolled like a swiss roll and put into a cloth and boiled, this was called a bacon-jack. The sweet variety of this dish was also enjoyed, fillings being jam, golden syrup or fruit, the one filled with currants or raisins was called a spotted-dick. Baked bread puddings were also a good stand-by and many a slice of cold bread pudding went into my father's lunch-time snack.

My mother made delicious dough-cakes, these were a treat. Butter was eaten only on Sundays or special days, at other times our bread was spread with jam, lard or dripping, the lard would be homemade from the pigs we had reared in the stye at the bottom of our garden and often seasoned with rosemary. Breakfast for the children of our house was a big bowl of hot Quaker Oats porridge followed by a thick slice of bread fried in bacon fat. Vegetables were usually plentiful and home grown in the garden or allotment.

I never knew my paternal grandmother; my mother's mother lived in a village six miles the other side of Banbury so I did not see her very often. However I remember that she once came to care for us when my mother was ill. My father had just killed a pig so the offal was used for our midday meal. I loathed to eat this. On this occasion my grandmother put a dish of chitterlings before me and I just would not eat them. My mother would have given me something else, but not my grandmother. She said that it was good, wholesome food and I would get nothing else until I had eaten it. I still refused so had no dinner. To my surprise and dismay it was put in front of me for my tea. I still refused to eat but my grandmother won in the end for the next day hunger forced me to eat this. That was the last time I ever ate pig's offal.

After that I disliked my grandmother intensely and avoided her as much as possible. One day, many years later I reminded my mother of this incident. My mother then told me that her father had died when she was nine years old and that her mother had worked twelve to eighteen hours a day to feed and clothe a family of four. She took in washing and in the summer months she worked in the fields from 5.0am until 8.0am then home to see that her children had their breakfast before going to school. She then worked again in the evening until it was dark when she would start to iron and mend the washing, often until after midnight. This made me realise what a very hard life my grandmother had lived. Like my parents, she never had a holiday. It also made me realise why she refused to let me waste what she considered good, wholesome food.

Like most other men my father grew the vegetables we required, some of my earliest recollections are of seeing him digging and planting in our garden. The old saying 'A penny saved is a penny gained' was certainly the motive behind the growing of vegetables. Of course, there was no money to buy fertilizers (although the pigs and chicken certainly helped!) and insecticides were of the home devised, not commercial variety. In the garden cleanliness became the keynote. No rubbish was left lying around to become the breeding place for pests and diseases. There were many tried and tested remedies; for grubs on gooseberry or currant a bonfire was made of dry sticks and weeds, this on the windward side of the bushes, the smoke would drift across and the grubs, not liking the smoke, would roll up and fall to the ground where they were collected and destroyed. We had a garden syringe, a heavy brass affair. This would be filled with soapy water from the washing or bath tub and used to spray away aphids and caterpillars. This did not injure the plants, neither did it leave any residue or chemical in the food, indeed, that may be why my memories of the vegetables and fruit are that they always tasted delicious. As children we all loved to see butterflies and moths but they were not so popular with the gardeners. My father always declared they were the 'worst enemy' in the garden, a single insect could deposit enough eggs to over-run a patch of plants with caterpillars, so they were caught and destroyed. Birds, too, were not welcome during the fruit season, during the time when the buds were opening they were dusted by a liberal helping of old chimney soot. You must realise that soot was a very plentiful commodity in those days, every house was warmed by an open fire or kitchen range on which cooking was also done, water was also heated on the range or fire. Soot is unpalatable to birds so this treatment prevented damage to the bursting flower buds, it was easy to do, didn't cost anything and didn't harm the blossoms or leaves in the early stages of growth, in time it was washed off by the rain.

Wasps and blow flies were also prime targets, every queen wasp caught and killed in early spring saved the annoyance of a nest later in the year. Father used to kill slugs and snails by taking large cabbage leaves, heating them until quite soft, then rubbing them with unsalted lard or dripping. These leaves were placed near the slug and snail infestations and were soon covered with these insects, the leaves were then gathered up and the whole lot destroyed. Some gardeners would try to have a resident hedgehog in their strawberry patch, these little creatures are great eaters of slugs and snails. Another insecticide used in those days was made from adding paraffin to soft soap and then diluting with water, whilst charcoal mixed with water was about the cheapest disinfectant used. Incidentally, trays filled with a thin layer of freshly heated wood charcoal were used to deodorize or reduce offensive smells in houses. The charcoal was made red hot and placed on non-inflammable trays which were then cooled slightly and placed in the room. Another, perhaps more pleasant way of deodorizing rooms was by burning a few sprigs of lavender. Charcoal was also invaluable in the garden, it was finely powdered and used when planting seeds, this is something which is still done today, it sweetens the soil.

The kitchen garden was considered one of the most important parts of the domestic economy, whatever its size or situation. Even tiny plots were cultivated and many gardeners tried hard to make the plots ornamental as well as practical and productive. Much very hard work was expended on working the soil for the benefit of a good crop, and attention to the land meant a better crop and the difference between having plenty of vegetables for the family or being short through the winter. Of course, there was plenty of stable manure too, and a load could often be obtained for a few hours of work for the farmer during haymaking or harvest. With the pig and fowl manure which was usually available the soil was kept in good heart and fertile. The old saying that what comes from the land should be returned to the land was a saying people believed in. We used to have three heaps of rubbish in the garden, one which included household scraps was there to rot down and be used as compost, one was for things which would burn, the ashes would be sprinkled around, the third heap was for old tins which would eventually be taken to a nearby sand pit, when the pit was full it would be levelled off and covered with soil. Old rags and bottles were saved for collection by 'The Windmill Man' who came round the village with a little truck. For a couple of clean bottles or some clean rags we would get a little paper windmill on a stick.

Most men also had allotments which were rented in plots of half to two chains. Having a large family my father rented a two chain plot. As we had a large garden he used the allotment for just two crops, one chain was used for barley and one for potatoes. These crops would be alternated, after the potatoes were lifted the ground would be prepared for the spring sowing of barley, the barley plot would be dug and manured in the late autumn or early winter ready for the planting of the potato crop next spring. The barley would be cut with a scythe, tied into little bundles and stacked into small ricks which would be thatched or covered with a tarpaulin until the barley could be threshed. Each little rick of barley would be taken to the threshing machine, its owner's name being attached to it although most men stood and watched their crop being thrashed. The estate cart and horse were loaned free of charge for carrying the sacks of corn and

19

the straw to their owner's home. The straw would be used to bed down the pig and then, with the manure, returned to the land the next year.

The sacks of corn would be sent to the mill, either at Souldern or Clifton, two nearby villages and the resultant meal used to fatten the pig for killing. A few cottagers grew wheat instead of barley and so had home grown flour for bread baking. The villagers were also allowed to go 'gleaning' by most of the local farmers, this meant going into the fields after the sheaves of corn had been gathered in, the loose ears of corn were collected and many a fat cockerel for Christmas has been fed on these 'gleanings'. This was often a task for the entire family and great was our satisfaction at a goodly harvest.

The older villagers would look at the weather with anxious eye when it was harvest time. There were no official weather forecasts in those days but many an old stager would be adept at foretelling the weather, and without the aid of satellite pictures, too. If the dew was particularly plentiful on the grass after a fine day it was a sign of another fine day to follow. If there was no dew and no wind then rain would be expected. The old saying 'Red sky at night shepherds' delight' was only partially true. A red evening portended a fine day to follow unless the redness spread upward from the horizon when winds, or rain or both would be expected. This type of weather was also expected if the morning was red 'Red sky in the morning, shepherds' warning'. It was said that a raining sky tinged with sea-green would mean the rain would increase but if tinged with deep blue it would become showery. Fast increasing clouds meant heavy rain and perhaps thunder, and the wives would gather in the washing! Clouds formed like fleeces but dense in the middle and bright towards the edge would mean frost with hail, snow or rain and tender plants would be shrouded in straw for protection and the house windows shut tight. High clouds looking like locks of wool meant wind and rain to follow and general cloudiness with small, black clouds scudding below inevitably was interpreted as rain of a lasting nature. In the summer two currents of clouds were always assumed to mean rain and probably thunder. Of course, some old fogeys 'told' the weather by their aches and pains, when I was a small child there was an old man in the village whose painful feet invariably forecast rain.

In the early part of the century home cures for both humans and animals were the norm. There was no National Health Service and the doctor was called only when matters were serious; later on there were doctors' clubs into which a small weekly payment was made, but in those early days of the century even the man in regular work hesitated to use the services of a doctor. Wages were low, as a skilled sawyer my father earned 19/- (95p) a week, carters and cowmen received just 15/- (75p) and the pay for women was even lower, an expense of the doctor could create a real problem. We were lucky in Aynho, Dr Saunders was a very good doctor and, like many other doctors of his day, would sometimes 'forget' to send in a bill to the very poor people of the village. Often such people hesitated to send for him until it was too late. Sometimes the bill would be settled by barter, a ham or a flitch of bacon being taken in lieu of money. My sister, being a semi-invalid, frequently needed the help of the doctor whose bill was often paid by the efforts of my father and brother who would go to the doctor's house to saw logs. Dr Saunders lived at the old Grammar School House and would drive around in a dog cart. This was a two-wheeled carriage with seats back to back and is so called because originally sporting dogs were carried inside the box on the cart. My brother once told me that he had heard the doctor ask my father how much the saw cutting was worth. When my father said he didn't know the doctor replied 'If you sent for me I should know what to charge you', so they agreed that my father and brother should cut as many logs as they thought would be fair. It was with sadness that the villagers lost Dr Saunders when he left the village in 1913 and it was then that Sir Fairfax and Lady Cartwright took up residence in the old Grammar School and changed its name to 'The Grammar House'.

21

Most of the old remedies were simple and most were effective. If a cut or graze showed any sign of inflammation no time was lost in applying a poultice of bread and hot water or of hot linseed meal. If these were not available then very hot flannels would be applied. Linseed oil or olive oil would be mixed with chalk and vinegar to make a compound about the consistency of honey and this was applied with a soft brush or a feather to scalds or burns. This was very soothing and the application would be renewed frequently. Of course, if the burn or scald was very bad, with a large area of open flesh the doctor or village nurse would be called. Often burns were just covered with wheat flour, the extruded fluid formed a paste and excluded air. Boils would be 'brought to a head' by the application of warm poultices of camomile flowers or onions; nettle stings could be cured by applying rosemary, sage or dock leaves. Chapped hands were a very serious problem for the girls and women whose hands were frequently in water and using harsh soaps. A very soothing ointment used to be made which also served for broken chilblains. One pint of Sweet Oil was heated slowly with three ounces of Venice Turpentine, half a pound of hog's lard and three ounces of bee's wax, these were stirred with a wooden spoon until all began to simmer when it was set aside and allowed to cool. It was fit to use as soon as it became cool but seemed to increase in effectiveness the longer it was kept so large batches were made up.

The barbed sting of a bee is left in the wound so speed in removing it was essential, my mother was adept at removing these stings by pressing on the wound with a watch key after which she sucked the wound to remove the last of the poison. For wasp stings she always applied sweet oil, onion juice or she rubbed the wound with the blue bag from her wash tub. I was often stung because I spent so much time out doors, indeed, when I started working in the gardens I was once very badly stung as my work took me very near several bee hives.

In those days we wore heavy boots so blistered feet were often a problem, one home remedy was a mixture of spirits with tallow from a candle. Of course, boots were 'broken in' before regular use. For the heavy outdoors working boots the menfolk would use a greasy substance called dubbin which both softened the leather and helped to keep the boots waterproof. It was the custom to wear the boots for an hour or two each evening before taking them for full time wear. My father told us that one day he remarked to his workmate that he would be glad to get home and take off his new boots as they were blistering his feet whereupon the man replied 'You should be like me, I always wear mine for a fortnight before I put them on'.

So my early childhood was one of simple pleasures, homely food and little luxury. A loving and caring mother and a hard working father meant that my lot was probably better than that of many another youngster of the day. But then I was three, and that meant school.

Chapter 3

Schooldays and boyhood

Like the majority of village children I started classes at the Aynho Infant School in my fourth year. At the time, the Infant School was a lean-to structure on the side of the Adult School which had been designed by Mr Clement Millard and built on the site of an old barn on Barton's Farm. Most villages of any size had an Adult School at which the grown-ups studied a variety of subjects, usually in evening classes. These classes were for those things which might prove helpful in our future life – for instance how to prevent, and what to do in case of accidents. We also learnt what to do in case of fire, in those days so much wood was burnt that there was always a danger of fire in the chimney, and should that happen a thoroughly soaked piece of thick material should be nailed to the mantlepiece so as to cover completely the opening; the fire would usually go out by itself. On some old mantlepieces there was a knob at each end on which the material could be tied. We also carried on with the 3 R's and the last hour on Friday evening was given over to physical training which included practising for the Morris Dance Team, boxing, etc.

Miss Oakey taught the infants, which at the beginning of the century included me, in what was called the Little Room, while in the Big Room were the first and second standards taught by a Miss Braithwaite (nicknamed Mollie) the third, fourth and fifth standards being taught by the headmaster Mr Hill.

But back to the Infant School, the seats were in three tiers, rather like an arena so by one look the teacher could see the entire class, there was no hiding behind the boy in front. I'm afraid Mr Hill was not popular with the children, he was elderly and near to retirement when I first went to school. When he retired and left the village we children treated the day like a holiday! Looking back I realise his life was probably not particularly easy. The new headmaster was Mr Pollard a very different type of man who was universally liked. I admired and respected him and, after I left school at thirteen Mr Pollard still took an interest in me and allowed me to attend the evening classes he held for the over fifteens. It was partly through the good offices of Mr Pollard that I was fortunate enough to become a gardener's boy at Aynho House, but I am jumping ahead. . . . My schooldays were full of new interests. I remember how I first learned the alphabet and how to count. Our letters were learnt by copying on to a slate, this was about ten inches by seven inches and was enclosed in a wooden frame. Our 'pencils' were also of slate and made a most horrid screeching noise, especially when drawing a straight line. These slate pencils broke easily so were attached to the frame of the slate by a piece of string to prevent them from falling to the ground if dropped. I can still, in memory, hear the appalling noise of a classroom of children screeching away with their 'slates'. Counting we learned by the use of an abacus, a wooden frame with wires stretched across and wooden balls attached, these were moved along the wires and counted.

Every morning school started with the calling of the register and then about thirty minutes of religious teaching, indeed, this teaching was considered more important than the 3 R's. I remember we were first taught simple prayers and stories. The first hymn I learned was 'What a friend we have in Jesus' which is still a favourite of mine. This was closely followed by a learning of 'All things bright and beautiful' and 'There is a green hill far away', lovely old, tuneful hymns which somehow are much more dear than the modern 'with-it' hymns I sometimes hear today. At a very early age every child was expected to know The Lord's Prayer, The Belief and the Ten Commandments. By the time schooldays were over one was expected to know these and other prayers and also the General Thanksgiving.

Aynho had (and still has) only the one place of worship, St Michaels and All Angels Church, when I was young there was only one Roman Catholic family in the village, that of Mr Bennett the butler at Aynho Park House. His children did not come to school until 9.30 to avoid taking part in the religious teaching that started the day, and even then I wondered at the attitudes of the different religions towards each other's interpretation of the gospels. Although there was no antagonism towards the Bennett Boys, nevertheless they seemed to be 'different' and very much kept to themselves, of course, some of this may have been due to the snobbery of the day, after all, the butler was a pretty exalted being!

There were exciting days that we looked forward to with great anticipation. Two in particular which are no longer observed, and more is the pity. One was St George's Day and the other Empire Day. These were celebrated by marching round the playground and, with great gusto and, I fear, questionable tunefulness, singing such patriotic songs as Rule Britannia and Land of Hope and Glory, Hearts of Oak and The British Grenadiers. Then came the National Anthem and we saluted the flag, then, joy of joys, the rest of the day was declared a holiday! I wonder why, in retrospect, those extra days were always bright and sunny?

We also celebrated 29 May, Oak Apple Day, again, a day few still remember. It seems funny to me now that staunchly Republican Aynho should, some two hundred and fifty years later, celebrate the escape of King Charles II by hiding in an oak tree. On that day we would scour the oak trees to try to find an oak apple which we would proudly wear pinned to our jerseys. The escape of the King was after the Battle of Worcester and our imagination would tell us that this oak or that one was 'the actual tree'! Boyhood imagination is a wonderful thing!

So memories of my childhood and schooldays are a kaleidoscope of changing patterns, of people and places, of customs and ideas, of joys and of less joyous occasions. Sometimes I sit and think of those days, of the way we spoke, of the strange and sometimes incomprehensible names we had for various things and of pronunciations. I remember three-pence was never anything but 'thrupence', not quite the 'thruppence' used elsewhere. Ants were 'piss emmetts', I never knew why. I remember asking an older man why ants were so called, the answer is with me still, 'I don't know, and why ask such bloody silly questions?' Of course, we did not have the radio or television, or indeed the cinema in my early days so did not have their influence on our way of speech, 'do not' was usually 'dunt', 'something' was almost always 'summat'.

Again, I remember some of my old playmates and companions, I remember funny little ways and incidents and the tricks we used to play. I chuckle to myself remembering the answer my pal Teddy gave to a man who asked him if he knew the time, Teddy replied 'It's about now in High Wycombe'. I remember Jim Garrett who used to arrive at school in such a tired and sleepy state that he frequently fell asleep over his book or slate. The school sent a message to Jim's parents complaining that the boy was not getting enough sleep (a frequent occurrence when a child had to help the family finances by working before or after school) it was then discovered that, with the aid of a straw, Jim had been drinking from a barrel of homemade wine and was not suffering from lack of sleep but was tipsy! Another boy was Walt William. His boots were heavy and had been treated with grease to soften the leather. Mr Pollard complained that his boots were dirty and told him to clean them. Of course, polish does not take on top of grease so the boots remained unpolished. On his way round the class on the next day the master noticed the boots and complained that the boy had not obeyed his order to polish them. 'No,' said Walt, 'I haven't polished 'em but I've 'graced' 'em.'

One boy, no matter how much tuition he received could not master even simple arithmetic. One day he was asked to do a simple sum. 'If your father had £10.00 and kept £5 for himself and gave the rest to your mother, what would she have?' The idea of his father having £10.00 was so funny that the boy replied 'She'd have a fit'. Inevitably we played 'April Fool' tricks, once someone in the top class said 'Please Sir there's someone at the door', of course there wasn't but the master looked, he distinctly heard several voices saying 'April Fool', whereupon he caned the entire class, boys and girls alike. The punishment was soon forgotten and we only remembered the fun of making the master an 'April Fool'.

We played the usual tricks of childhood both on each other and on adults and woe betide anyone who upset us, we would have revenge! Joe Watt's father was one who fell foul of some of us. The Watts family lived in a cottage with a stone flagged passage leading from the front door to the rear of the house, above the front door was a flat stone some three feet by two feet built out from the wall to form a porch. One dark night several of us decided to repay some imagined offence so, as I was the smallest and lightest I was hoisted on to the stone porch, I reached under and, with a long stick knocked the door whilst my mates hid some distance away but with a view of the porch. Mr Watts opened the door and peered out, of course, he couldn't see anyone so went along and opened the back door with the same result. Giving him time to settle down again by his fireside I again knocked, again he came along and looked out. By now he had realised what was happening so did not go right back but shut the door and waited just inside it. Again, after a short while I knocked on the door which was immediately flung open, 'Got you, you young buggers' shouted our victim slashing out with a riding whip and he rushed down the path the whip flaying from side to side. My mates took to their heels leaving me crouched on the porch praying that Mr Watts wouldn't look up as he returned, fortunately for me, he didn't and I scrambled down and ran as fast as my shaking legs would carry me.

Another of our favourite childhood tricks was to tie stout pieces of cord to the door handles of adjacent houses, this was done with great stealth and controlled excitement. We would leave about three inches of slack, then two of us would knock the two doors simultaneously and run for cover. It was a great joy to listen to the comments at the tug-of-war game that ensued! A favourite place for this pastime was the Charlton Road where every other house was divided by a passage along which we could creep. We never left enough slack for the occupants to be able to cut the cord so they would have to climb from a window, we of course, making sure we were at a safe distance!

We often played football using a pig's bladder for a ball. When pig killing time came round we would offer to help by holding the pig or fetching pails of water or any other chore, anything to enable us to get the bladder. We would allow it to dry when the skin became hard. Inflated this made an excellent football, the only sort we were able to have! This game could lead to trouble. There was one old man who, if the football came anywhere near him, would burst it or take it away. We decided to teach him a lesson. One night we waited until it was really dark and then climbed on to his roof via his garden shed, over the chimney we placed a thick, wet sack. Soon we were rewarded by the sight of the man coming out coughing and rubbing his eyes and, eventually, we saw him carry the live coals out from his grate. Next morning, of course, he saw the sack and found the cause of his smoking fire. I think he also realised who the culprits were and why it was done as he never tried to interfere with our game again.

Opposite our house was the blacksmith, I spent many a

happy hour watching him work and was even allowed to help by pumping the bellow for his fire. In the late 1800s the blacksmith had been Mr Taylor whose daughter was mentally retarded so the windows were barred and the doors secured to prevent her from getting out. Mr Taylor took an assistant named Teddy Mobbs and it was he who was blacksmith when I was young. My earliest memories of Teddy go back to my very early childhood, even as young as two years old I used to at first sit on a little stool on the door step of 86 and when I grew a little older on the grass bank by the side of the house to watch the shoeing of horses so you can imagine my joy when I was allowed to hold the horses' heads and later to pump the bellows, even though I had to stand on a box to reach the handles! Teddy Mobbs had another claim to fame. He was the drummer of the Aynho Bugle Band of the Local Volunteer Force in the First World War. After the smithy assistant was called up to join the forces the older men took to going along to the smithy to help. No money was paid for this help but it was warm, the men could gather to talk and discuss the latest news from the war fronts and, best of all, Teddy Mobbs provided copious supplies of free beer!

It was during one of these sessions that one of the men reported that he had a raging toothache and asked Teddy to pull it out as it would save him the expense of going to the doctor. The extraction was done in a rather crafty way. A piece of strong, thin, wire was tied around the tooth with the other end round the anvil. In the fire was a piece of red hot iron, picking this up with his pincers Teddy advanced on the 'patient' who jumped backwards, the tooth was out! No doubt the gum was sterilized by a good, long draught of beer!

I also liked to watch the wheelwrights. Mr Baughan and his assistant Mr Clements were extremely skilled in repairing and making things of wood. It was with considerable pleasure that I watched them making a farm wagon. The wheels were made in sections, the spokes being shaped using a spokeshave and finally, the blacksmith made and fitted iron rims to the wheels.

There were many other men of the village who were true craftsmen. The Secull men were stonemasons, their skills being used to maintain the stone buildings of the village and the big wall which surrounded the Park. This wall was over five miles long and between six and seven feet high so needed considerable attention. There were deer in the Park and these will quickly find a gap so great care was taken to ensure the security of the wall. The Secull family had their share of tragedy. In those days the 'privy' was usually at the end of the garden and one dark night the Secull daughter had gone to the privy and had lit a candle. A few minutes later her mother heard screams and found the girl on fire, her nightdress was blazing. The flames were beaten out but not before the girl had suffered dreadful burns, her hands were reduced to stumps, she died some two years later never having recovered from the accident. My sister Ethel was subsequently named after this girl who was the daughter of one of my mother's greatest friends. Another member of the family had been found drowned in one of the large underwater tanks near the Park House.

It was to Mrs Secull that we children would go for our midday meal if my mother had to be away from home, or if she was ill. I have many memories of running up the Skittle Alley with a message to Mrs Secull from my mother.

Of course, there were many other skilled men employed on the Aynho estate and many of these often worked with a watching gallery of small boys. One man would be in charge of the painting and decorating of the houses, then there was the plumber. During my childhood the thatcher was kept busy but gradually the thatched roofs gave way to slates. The thatch came from straw from the estate as did the willows for making hurdles and the osiers for baskets. There was one man, his name escapes me now, who had the responsibility for all the drains and made extra cash for himself by emptying the closets, as the privies were then called. For this purpose he used a long scoop. The privies were usually at the bottom of a garden, as far from the house as possible and they needed frequent emptying, not a particularly pleasant task. With a family the size of ours it was, of necessity, an almost daily task so my father obtained his own scoop for this job and so avoided paying the drains man.

Mr Gibbs did all the leather work, he repaired the horse tack and did much of the village cobbling. Of course, many men did the shoe and boot repairing for their families, some did it much better than others. A small iron cast was used by some men, this had feet shapes of different sizes, shapes rather like the three legged sign of the Isle of Man.

Some men had more than one job, for example the sexton did his church work which included keeping the churchyard tidy and digging the graves but he also trimmed the wicks and filled the oil reservoirs of the six lamps which illuminated the village. Of course, all estate men were called to help out for certain jobs, for harvest time, for collecting ice from the lake for the ice house and any emergency. When the Oxford Canal froze the Nell Bridge Farm provided a horse and an iron boat to break the ice on that section of the canal which passed through the estate. For some reason this part of the canal was always called The Cut.

There were village customs which served to brighten our lives, and which compensated us for our otherwise strict upbringing, many have sadly been discontinued over the years, a great pity this, they added colour to English rural life. One event to which we eagerly looked forward was the Sunday School Treat. This was held annually at the Rectory grounds and we had games and races and a splendid tea. Another event was the May Day celebration when a large garland of flowers was carried round the village followed by the May Queen and her attendants, the rest of the children followed singing May songs. The May Queen was a very much sought after position, she usually wore a white dress with a garland of flowers on her head, and she carried a bouquet of flowers.

Of course the really big day was that of the Annual Flower Show which was held in the Park grounds and in which all the villagers joined. The menfolk displayed the results of their skill in growing fruit, flowers and vegetables whilst their wives and the other ladies exhibited cakes and jams, chutneys, pickles, needlework and knitting. Children too were encouraged to exhibit, for days before the event both girls and boys would be searching the area for queen wasps, a prize being given for the collector of the largest number. The boy working in the warm greenhouses had rather an advantage, warm greenhouses in early spring are very attractive to queen wasps! There were classes for exhibits of wild flowers, for drawing and painting and for needlework.

However, the main attraction for the children was that this was a holiday, as a bonus there was the possibility of winning a penny or two in the competition. Beside the usual flat races there were egg and spoon races, three-legged races, sack races, thread the needle and others. If I remember correctly the winner of each race won threepence, the second twopence and the third one penny. But remember, the local sweet shop did a brisk trade in ha'peths of dolly mixtures, bulls-eyes, aniseed balls and liquorice allsorts. Great favourites were the sherbet fountains, yellow paper-covered tubes of cardboard containing dry sherbert powder which was sucked up through a tube of liquorice, and the sherbet dabs, flat lumps of a toffee-like substance on a stick in a packet of sherbet, these, with the liquorice strings, liquorice pipes, packets of sugar cigarettes all cost just one half penny, so the winners of threepence could really indulge themselves!

One of the most amusing and most watched events at the Flower Show was the 'catch the pig'. For this a young pig was greased all over and put into a pen about four yards square. It would become the property of the first person to catch it and carry it out. The event was open to all and was very attractive to the young men of the village, few ladies would risk their finery! Anyone wearing gloves or trying to wipe the grease from the piglet would face immediate disqualification and a certain amount of tut-tutting from the spectators as it was considered extremely unsporting and was seldom attempted.

The Morris Dancers also performed and as a young man I took part in this. We wore the traditional dress of the Morris Men, white flannel trousers with small bells sewn on garters and worn below the knee, white shirts, white straw hats decked with flowers and ribbons and a white handkerchief in each hand although for one or two dances staves were used instead of the handkerchiefs, one such dance was called Bean Setting. All these dances had been handed down for generations and it is so good to see that there are still men determined to keep alive the old, country tradition of Morris Dancing.

Another favourite competition was 'swiping the ham'. A fifteen to twenty pound ham would be suspended from the branch of a tree by a stout piece of cord so that it was about seven or eight feet above the ground. The contestant would stand on a line six yards away from the ham, he would be blindfolded and turned around three times whereupon he was allowed three swipes at the ham. Help from the spectators was not allowed and it was surprising how few managed to hit the prize. At the end of the competition there was an elimination contest to decide the winner leaving someone with a very nice prize to take home. The competitive games always ended with a tug-of-war contest between Souldern and Aynho. I'm afraid Souldern nearly always won, they had a big advantage – the twenty stone men of the Titcombe family who were always on the end of the Souldern rope.

After the competitions ended the ramp which had been constructed over the wall to the parkland below was opened and we streamed over to the attractions which we boys and girls loved most of all, the roundabouts, swings and side-shows. There were hoop-la stalls, and stalls selling sweetmeats, there was music and flare lights and we were transported into an exciting world. One thing in great demand by the boys was a tube similar to a toothpaste tube which was filled with water. We would chase the girls and squirt water down their backs – such excitement for the price of one halfpenny. There were little saw-dust filled balls wrapped in paper and on the end of a thin elastic which we used to throw to hit the girls, the elastic had a boomerang effect and the ball came back to our hand, but I believe these cost a whole penny.

The grounds around had been transformed into fairyland by hundreds of coloured lights which would be lit as night descended. They were, in fact, no more than painted jam jars with a candle inside, these were lit using long tapers and great was our joy when, as older boys, we were entrusted with the tapers. Dancing on the lawn to a silver band continued until midnight when festivities closed for another year, but, oh how we enjoyed it all!

Another attraction was the meet of the fox hounds. The hunt gathered on the green outside the Cartwright Arms public house to partake of the usual stirrup cup. There was much running around of the children, much sagacious comment by the older villagers on the likely run, or the quality of the horses. When the hounds moved off we followed them on foot vying with each other to open gates in the path of the riders and possibly earn a welcome copper or two. Another way we could earn a penny was when the local farmers gathered to shoot the young rooks from the belts of trees around the park. Local sportsmen would gather at Park House around 4.0pm and the older boys would rush from school anxious to offer service as carriers of the ammunition satchels. Some men were known to be more generous than others and everyone wanted to be chosen by them. Many were the 'accidental' trippings and even fights to settle who would 'carry' for these gentlemen. Boys not lucky enough to be chosen would rush to collect the fallen birds, for each one collected they received one half penny.

At one time Aynho had a sale-yard but this was eventually closed and the business transferred to the Banbury Cattle Market. During holidays or on Saturday a boy could earn a shilling for helping to drive the cattle to Banbury which, in those days, was held in the streets of the town with the cattle being kept from the pavements by iron railings. A boy lucky enough to be so engaged would usually take a friend with him and the two lads would stay the whole day in Banbury for, if the cattle were not sold, they would have to be driven back. Sometimes the farmer would buy other cattle and these would have to be escorted back to the farm. If there was nothing to drive back the boys would try to get a ride back home with the farm cart which might have been used to take pigs or sheep or chicken to the market. If no ride was available they would either walk the six miles home or, if they felt they could afford it, they would pay two pence to ride home on the carrier's cart. The boys took their own food for the day. A couple of thick slices of bread spread with home-made jam, or lard flavoured with rosemary leaves might be accompanied by a couple of hard boiled eggs, whilst drink was a bottle of lemonade.

Many women sent eggs to the market, they were plentiful as most people kept some hens but many women bought extra to preserve for the winter, they used to call this 'putting down' the eggs. There were two methods used to preserve eggs. In one, clean eggs were put into an earthenware jar into which had been put a half bushel of quick lime, one pound of salt, and a quarter pound of cream of tartar. Water was added and the whole thing stirred to a consistency whereby an egg would float with its top just showing above the liquid. The other method was to paint the eggs with a solution of gum arabic and pack them in dry charcoal dust. I once heard of a method used in some places where the eggs were coated with lard but I do not remember ever seeing this done in my home. Another easy way for anyone who kept hens and had a cool dry cellar was to get a piece of inch board, one foot wide and two and a half feet long and in this bore about fifty holes one and a half inches in diameter, then nail thin strips of wood round the edges to serve as a ledge. As fast as the eggs were laid they were placed in these holes with the small end downwards and they would keep fresh for weeks.

There was still another way in which we could earn a little money. As I have said, in the early days of this century most houses were thatched with straw. Birds, especially the house sparrow caused a great deal of damage in making nests under the eaves and gable ends. So to reduce the damage the older boys were encouraged to borrow ladders and rob the nests. For every egg taken to the estate office on Friday evening at 5.00pm the sum of one farthing would be paid, for every young bird the payment was one half penny and a whole penny for an adult bird.

We also earned money catching rats. A penny would be paid for every rat tail. We caught the rats in the pig styes, chicken runs and from the rick-yard at threshing time, this latter was particularly rewarding if the ricks had been built on a layer of faggots, straw or hay, we rarely found rats under the ricks which had been raised off the ground by staddle stones.

Just before Christmas came another welcome chance to earn some money. During the latter part of December a large stock of coal was carted to the yard opposite the Cartwright Arms. This coal was one of the Squire's Christmas gifts to the village people. One and a half hundredweights would be given to each man and woman, one hundredweight to each child up to school leaving age and five hundredweights to each of the almshouse residents. The coal was weighed and put into heaps for each family depending on its size. Boys and girls would queue with wheelbarrows or home-made trucks to take the coal to its new owners, for this they received one penny a hundredweight.

Men would help in carting the coal from the wharf yard and in unloading the barges which brought the coal and in recognition of this help they were allowed to drag the canal the whole length of the wharf for coal which may have dropped into the water. This was quite a concession and a considerable amount of coal could be salvaged.

I remember I used to spend my earnings (or some of them) in the little sweet shop kept by Miss Millard. Often I would have only a farthing to spend and I used to spend this on a sugar mouse, a sherbet dab or a chocolate watch, very rarely did I have a whole penny to spend. I was one of Miss Millard's favourites and had many little extras. In a small way I was able to pay back these little kindnesses when Miss Millard left her shop and went to live in one of the almshouses. I often visited her doing little jobs around the house, or running errands or shopping, sometimes I would spend the whole day with her and she would talk to me of 'olden days'. One very hot and sultry day I was having tea with her when there was a terrible thunderstorm. Even though it was a very hot day there was a little fire as this was Miss Millard's only means of boiling a kettle. The door was open and as we sat talking there was suddenly a terrific crash. I remember seeing the fire snuffed out like a candle and a bluish haze rush past between me and Miss Millard and out of the door. The next thing I remember was being back at my home with a dreadful headache and feeling very sick. I was put to bed and it was not until next morning that I learnt that Miss Millard was not harmed in any way and that a fire ball had struck the chimney stack splitting it in half and smashing slates as it bounded to the ground. Men who had been sheltering in the barn opposite said that they had seen the fire ball strike, they also teased me about the way I shot out of the house as if the devil were after me. For many years after, although not actually afraid of thunder, I had a peculiar feeling, a curious feeling of loss if a storm threatened and did not materialise.

There is another reason why I remember Miss Millard.

One day when I went to visit her I was surprised to find a tall, bearded gentleman with her whom she introduced as her nephew. This surprised me as I had not known that she had any relative living. We had a talk together and I was promised a book from the nephew's library. He told me he prized this book and would send it to me only on condition that I promised to keep it as long as I lived. The book arrived just in time for my thirteenth birthday and I still have it. It is 10½ inches by 13½ inches and is the *Sunday Pictorial Book*, it has 416 pages, 206 of which have 1302 small pictures which are numbered and refer to Biblical subjects. There are pictures concerning the Psalms, one for each and many are prints from pictures by great masters – Raphael, Rubens, Leonardo da Vinci, Michelangelo, and many others. In the margin of the pictures there are notes and dates of nearly 150 years ago. In addition to the 416 pages of Bible history there are 10 illuminated maps of the Land of Canaan and 48 pages of The Scripture Atlas, Geography of the Holy Land. Page 30 of the text describes the terrible earthquakes in Syria in the year 1822. The latest date I can discover in the book is on page 14 – I quote – 'We shall await with impatience the more extended information which Mr Russegger must be prepared to give, and which is understood now (1844) on the point of publication.' This book, one of my most cherished possessions, has given me very many interesting hours and has more than compensated me for the little things I did for my old friend Miss Millard.

Moral standards were high in those far off days. If a young man got a girl 'into trouble' he was given the choice of either marrying the girl or leaving the village. The choice sometimes led to people leaving as responsibility was not always accepted, however, the attitudes rather changed after the First World War, and one such man who had been forced to leave did, in fact, finally return to the village and took the post of gardener at the Grammar House.

Mr Woolnough was the estate agent and wielded great influence over the village being arbiter in many disputes between estate workers. The six brothers of the Watts family rang the six church bells and one of them, James Watts, went into partnership with William Turner who had previously been gardener at the Rectory, they farmed a few acres and were always referred to as one, 'TURNERANDWATTS.' With their horses they helped on the estate carting manure and leaves or heavy loads from the station. Mr Turner drove around in a pony cart. The pony was rather high-spirited and whenever the opportunity occurred would run off. Such an opportunity once occurred when Mr Turner got out of the cart to open the gate to a field. The pony took off at a great rate and, on reaching the opposite side of the field, plunged through the hedge but the cart didn't go through the hedge and brought the pony to a sudden halt. With himself one side and the cart held firmly the other side of the hedge the pony received such a thrashing that he never attempted to run off again.

I mentioned Mr Woolnough as the estate agent but my memory of him is more concerned with our Boy Scouts troop, his son, Jim was our leader and through him we were able to acquire materials such as we would not have been able to afford. One of our most useful acquisitions being our truck cart which we understood to be a present from the Squire. I think it was made in Mr Baughan the wheelwright's shop and was constructed so that it could be taken apart and reassembled in a few minutes, the sides doubling in use as a ladder. I remember our first camping weekend, we pitched camp at the bottom of the park and the sides of the truck were used to form a bridge over the trout stream. Funds for our troop were raised at concerts and socials and the money used to buy our uniforms and camping equipment, we were the envy of troops in surrounding villages. We were also very lucky as we were allowed the use of a small, empty cottage which served as both our Scout headquarters and as our club where we could play games or read, especially in the winter months. When Mr Woolnough left to join the forces his sister carried on in his place until the war took more and more of the young men and the troop was disbanded and the headquarters closed.

I remember a morbid interest we boys displayed in watching the cattle being slaughtered, the hapless animal was imprisoned in a little shed next to the slaughter house, a strong rope was passed through a wooden block fixed to the floor then passed over the neck and tightened so that the head rested on the block, then, with one swift blow from a poleaxe the brain would be pierced, the animal would fall to the floor and its throat cut. However, the school master did not approve of this spectacle so Mr Oakey was asked not to slaughter animals until after 9.0am when we were all in school. Later the pole-axe gave way to the humane killer.

Stomachs concerned us greatly in those days and I well remember a special feast we enjoyed, this was something we called 'tuppenny cakes' (two-penny cakes). These were baked every Saturday afternoon, they were the most delicious dough cakes, two inches thick and about eight inches in diameter and, as the name suggests, these treats could be bought for just two pennies. Boys and girls would club together to raise the money to buy one of these cakes. In great anticipation we would go along to Checkley's, the little general store (which used to be a posting inn) and there buy a bottle of Spruce. This was a fizzy lemonade, we bought this in a glass bottle which was sealed with a glass marble which had to be pushed down the neck to enable the drink to be poured. The bottles were returnable, one farthing being the sum given, we seldom managed to get to the drink without breaking the bottle. Sometimes we would be financially sound so would buy a 'monster' bottle which cost a whole penny!

Earlier I mentioned Mr Oakey the slaughterer who was also butcher, baker, farmer selling milk, butter, eggs, corn, meal and even coal; he also has another claim to my memories. Facing the green square was Mr Oakey's barn whose doors, in our opinion, made an ideal goal, for our games of football. Unfortunately Mr Oakey did not share our view and he emphasised this point one day. He arrived carrying a thick cane causing our game to come to an abrupt halt. He always wore a black bowler hat tilted forward onto his forehead, so having stopped our game he turned to go back to his shop whereupon my brother Frank, who happened to have the ball, said 'Watch me knock old Oakey's hat off,' more by luck than judgement that is exactly what he did. Retribution was swift, Mr Oakey retrieved his hat and our ball which he pocketed. This was a real tragedy as tennis balls were very hard to come by but luck hadn't completely deserted us. The ball belonged to Jim Judd who was a nephew of the aforementioned general store owner Mrs Checkley. On hearing Jim's account of the incident, not perhaps the absolute truth, she came to the rescue with a verbal attack on Mr Oakey. To our utter amazement he returned the ball. This was rather surprising as he I suppose had the law on his side and, after all, he was the law for he was the senior Parish Constable. Aynho did not have a resident village policeman, the law enforcers in the village being two Parish Constables. They were issued with a pair of handcuffs and a truncheon and were chosen by the Watch Committee who chose two respected and reliable members of the community. There were no nominations for the posts, which were unpaid, the first indication to the 'lucky' persons chosen was when the names were posted to the Church door. This posting was a requirement to enable any parishioner to lodge a protest if he felt the chosen people were unfitted for the post. My brother Joe and Tom Oakey were the last two Parish Constables of Aynho.

The Howes family lived in a Tudor house which was a bakehouse. An outside staircase led up to a room where the flour was stored, being lowered for use in the bakehouse through a trap door by means of a canvas chute. With my friend I spent many hours during the winter months in this warm bakehouse hunting for crickets. In this upper room was a section in which were stored the bars of salt to be sold to the villagers for cooking purposes and pig killing time. The Howes family were also farmers and butchers but on a smaller scale than the Oakeys. The eldest son, Will managed the farm supplying the eggs and milk sold in their shop which was run by the daughter, Alice, who also made butter. Son John was the baker and butcher and later ran a hire service, first with a horse and cart and later with a car.

The brother with a cart was Will Howes, his cart was rather high and there was space underneath for his dog to run between the wheels. This dog was a cross sheepdog and collie and was Will's constant companion. One evening the dog went missing, Will was very worried as it was unknown for the dog to wander off. Next day the dog was found some miles away, it was still guarding the old coat Will had discarded the day before.

I have mentioned that John Howes was the baker and the butcher but on a smaller scale to the Oakeys, he gave another service to the villagers. Every Sunday morning John would prepare his oven to bake the Sunday joints for the majority of the village people. These dinners would be taken to him after 10.0am to be collected at 12.30. In my family the meal was taken in a large tin divided through the centre. On one side would be a Yorkshire pudding with a joint of beef or mutton suspended over it on a little iron stand. In the other side would be potatoes with a piece of pig meat or, sometimes, a sheep's head (which could be bought for about 6d – 2½p) above the potatoes. The cost of this cooking would be 2d or 3d (approx 1p) according to the size of the tin.

This same John Howes was in great demand at pig killing time, for 1/6d (7½p) he would kill the pig, hang it for a day and then cut it into suitable pieces. The charge for hiring the pulley for hoisting the pig for hanging was a further 6d (2½p) although if the pig was small the pulley wouldn't be required as the carcass could be lifted up to a hook attached to a stout beam. Another hire item was the lead in which the hams were cured, the charge for hiring was 6d but my father had his own lead and was always willing to lend it freely to neighbours when he was not using it himself. A lead is a wooden box without a lid. It was lined with lead and had a bung in a hole at the end. This box was filled with brine made from 1½ ounces of common soda and saltpetre to every 14 pounds of ham or bacon. The soda prevented hardness in the lean of the bacon, keeping it mellow all through, it also prevented rust. Pigs were a source of great pride, when they were killed they were weighed and the owner would boast that his pig had 'turned the scales' at 20 stone or that a ham had weighed between 40 and 60 pounds.

Every village seemed to have one or two people (usually boys!) who were a little simple, not quite village idiots perhaps but not quite as others. Two come to mind. One was a boy a little older than me. He was a big, strapping lad and this meant he was left alone pretty much, few would wish to provoke him. He lived with his parents and sister in one of the small cottages and might have stayed there but for one happening. He was found cutting the beak of a duck with an old penknife because 'The old bugger is scooping all the food and not letting the hens have any'. Soon after this episode the boy was sent to a 'home'; I think it was felt he might get too much for his elderly parents to manage and that the village might be safer if he were 'put away'. Of course, in those days there were not the same type of establishments we have today. The workhouse was the place that most simple people were sent to. The regime was not an easy one, the inmates wore coarse clothes and had to work very hard. Many of the women and girls were employed in the laundry, a hot, wet, steamy and horrible job. Most of the males worked in the very extensive gardens of the workhouse or were hired out to local farmers. I never did hear what happened to the boy of my story. The other story is of an incident that happened when I was about twelve. There was a young man called Alf who lived with his parents at Kings Sutton. One afternoon he came to visit his married brother who lived in a farm cottage between Kings Sutton and Aynho. Whilst he was there very heavy rain started, his sister-in-law thought it looked likely to continue so suggested that Alf should stay the night to avoid walking home in the rain. He was delighted to accept the invitation and a bed was made up in the spare room. Some time later the brother went to fetch Alf for his meal but there was no sign of him. Deciding that brother Alf had decided to go home after all the couple settled down to their meal, they had almost finished when there was a knocking at the door, there, rain streaming from him stood Alf, 'If I'm staying the night with you I need some pyjamas so I've been home to get them' he said.

It was about this time that the policeman of a nearby village was the source of a great deal of amusement. The village church had a thick yew walk to the church door and, in the dark evenings, worshippers were walking through and having their hats knocked off. It was decided that boys were to blame and that they were hiding in the bushes so the policeman volunteered to 'catch the varmints'. So the next Sunday he patrolled the walk and suddenly a shape swooped down on him and his hat was knocked off, he ran yelling out of the gate, sure that there was a ghost. Investigations by a bolder spirit with a lantern showed the culprit – a large barn owl.

Mr Bygrave farmed at Nell Bridge Farm and was also the landlord of the pub, the Cartwright Arms. Every Sunday morning he entertained all his workmen to breakfast after which the men swept the pathways around the public house and its yard, they also cleaned out the stables and the coach house but the task had to be completed before church-time, and when the task was done the ration of free beer was dispensed.

Many people had nick-names. Another Bygrave was a potato merchant so was named 'Tater Harry', his very tall son was 'Doughty Six-Foot'. I don't remember why some of the nicknames were chosen, some were obvious, the fat boy was Jumbo, the small man was Titch, but why were Pocketts, Punch, Slitherarm, Shuggy so called?

So my childhood ran its course. Few of my playmates are alive today and there is only one of my family left in Aynho. My cousin Harry Humphris is still there; he too worked for the Aynho estate being especially skilled in the art of dry stone walling, many of his walls still bear tribute to his skills.

However, there was one big influence in my childhood, and the childhood of all the village and that was the Church.

In July 1985 Aynho School finally closed its doors and after 140 years of educating local children its days were over. Now even the smallest pupils will have to travel to other villages – of course, since the 1930s the over elevens have gone to Kings Sutton or other schools. This is a very sad event, the life of a village should revolve round its school and churches and other institutions, now the pride in the village which the school fostered may be no more.

The trouble is that the estate was broken up and the sense of family disappeared, Aynho has become a dormitory for Oxford, Banbury and other larger places whilst many of the houses have become holiday or weekend homes. Older, more affluent people have bought the houses to renovate and restore but this has forced prices up to a level that the local young people cannot afford and so they have had to go elsewhere for their homes.

Gradually the pupils of the school will move away or die and there will be no links with something which paid such a part in village life. There are one or two of my schoolfriends still living in the village. Miss Gertie Garrett still lives in Little Lane, Aynho, she was our May Queen in 1913, and very pretty she was, too. Mrs Charlotte Czeppe is still a resident. She came as a young teacher to the school in 1930 and stayed teaching the Aynho young for over forty years, it must have been a very sad day for her when the school doors closed for the last time. Miss Nancy Stayton is another old friend of the village.

A commemorative service was held at the end of the final term, I feel it should have been a commiseration service. I understand that over two hundred people attended the service, many of them former pupils.

It was a day in June 1986 when we again went to Aynho in search of pictures to illustrate this book. We called on those three delightful octogenerians, Miss Gertie Garrett, Mrs Czeppe, youngest of the three,

46

and Miss Nancy Stayton. All three ladies were saddened that the school was up for sale; all felt it was another piece of the soul of the village which was being disposed of. They all mentioned that now there is a church but no rector, no school, only one shop and that the heart of the village had been lost when the Cartwrights moved from the village.

We went to look at the old school standing there, empty and forlorn. The notice said FOR SALE FOR RESIDENTIAL DEVELOP-MENT. Ted shook his head, 'Why couldn't they have used it for the benefit of the village or made it a museum?'

'I don't know, Ted, it does seem the obvious thing to do but I suppose someone, one day, will get an honour "for public service" for selling off all these bits of village heritage.'

Chapter 4

The Church

The Church of St Michaels and All Angels stands alongside Aynho Park House, it was founded in the fourteenth century during the reign of Edward III but all that remains of the original building is the tower. Near to the west door are niches thought to have contained statues, local legend says that these were mutilated by the Parliamentarian troops during the Civil War. Still visible over the west door are the remains of a statue of St Michael slaying the dragon, just the tail of the dragon being sole survivor, again, the Parliamentarians are held to have been responsible for this mutilation. A real conversation piece is the fact that the clock faces are off centre, the tower and these faces get a lot of attention from visitors and many ideas have been put forward for the reason for the position of the clock faces but it is all conjecture, no one really knows.

Like nearby Banbury, Aynho was a stronghold of Parliamentarianism so, during the Civil War the church, like nearby Aynho Park House was severely damaged. The main body of the church was rebuilt in 1723 in Grecian style, a local man, Edward Wing being the architect. Wing designed the new church to complement the Park House, indeed from the garden the church facade appears much more like a house. Edward Wing designed many London churches and his work at Aynho was largely financed by the benevolence of the then squire, Thomas Cartwright.

Before the church was built there were crosses in the village and it was from these crosses that monks and itinerant preachers would hold services. There is a cross in the churchyard now but it is believed to be of later origin.

Entering the church through the door in the tower the visitor is confronted by an unusual interior, there is no chancel. Box pews are arranged in four distinct groups, two at right angles to the others thus 'compensating' for the lack of a chancel. At the west end there is a gallery. In my young days the ceiling was of dark wood although a picture by an earlier Lady Cartwright dated 1846 shows the ceiling white plaster. In the 1960s failing roof trusses necessitated urgent repairs and a suspended ceiling was installed, again white.

After the death of the last squire, Richard Cartwright and his son Edward in 1954 a memorial was placed inside the church by his family. This is a wooden carving and carries a brass plaque of great interest, in French it is inscribed: 'A carving of Christ, given by Louis XIII to the sisters of the Hospital of St Louis to put in their chapel. The building seen at the bottom represents the old hospital begun under Henry IV in 1606 and finished under Louis XIII in 1619. This unusual carving came from the sale by the Augustine Sisters when they returned in 1906 and was bought by J. Coudre of Paris.'

There are other memorials in the church, many of members of the Cartwright family who were Lords of the Manor from 1616 until the mid-1950s. One other memorial is of very great interest as it lists the church rectors from Ralph de Dideto 1210 to William Gregory 1965. There are forty-six names on this tablet, some served only one year but Thomas Digby Cartwright held the living for forty-four years.

There are other memorials in the form of church regalia. An unusual altar frontal is the memorial to Euan Fleming which is reversible. During most of the year the red side is shown but during Lent and Advent it is reversed showing a white frontal embroidered with a crown of thorns. The altar cross is a recent addition having been given in 1972 by William and Justine Ashby in memory of Richard Ashby who died in Australia, aged thirty-two years. The lectern is in the shape of a pelican, ancient belief was that the pelican pecked her breast to feed her young and was used to symbolise the redemption of man by the shedding of Christ's blood.

A sad reflection on modern times is that the church plate is no longer kept there but is brought out for major festivals only. Three of these pieces are of special interest, a Charles II alms dish of solid silver, a flagon simply decorated with a reeded band and marked that it was made by Joseph Allen and Mordecai Fox in 1730, and an Elizabethan communion cup, also of pure silver this is over 10 inches high and bears the mark '1603, Aynho'.

Like all village children I attended Sunday School and church with great regularity. As a child I was fascinated by the clock, the mechanism for this clock is on the first floor of the tower and is signed 'Ed. Hemins, Bister Fecit 1740.' The clock is now wound automatically but when I was young there were weights which fell through two stories of the tower and had to be wound every four days, a sight which we children liked to watch. The carillion was installed in 1913 amid great excitement in the village. It is a pin movement and plays seven tunes, one for each day of the week. On Sunday it plays 'We love the place O God', Monday is 'God moves in a Mysterious way', Tuesday 'Life let us Cherish', Wednesday's tune is 'At the name of Jesus', Thursday, for some reason is not a hymn but 'The bluebells of Scotland', Friday is 'Sweet the moments, rich in blessing', whilst Saturday is another well-loved song, 'Home sweet Home'. Local theory was that Saturday's tune was chosen to remind the men to go home and not spend their wage packets in the Cartwright Arms!

The bells of Aynho Church were always of interest to me. In 1551 there were only three bells and a sanctus bell, it is not known when the three became six but in 1870 two more were added making Aynho and nearby Kings Sutton the only two eight-bell towers in South Northamptonshire. During the 1800s whilst there were still only six bells, these were rung by six brothers of the Watts family, Titus, Thomas, Timothy, William, John and James which led to the little rhyme:

> Tite, Tom, Tim
> Will, Jack, Jim.

My friend Joe Watts was fond of telling me this little story about his ancestors. My own interest probably stemmed from the fact that my father was a bellringer and tolled the Rector's Bell, which rang out every Sunday morning at exactly 9.0am except on the first Sunday of the month when it was tolled by the sexton at 8.0am for the Communion Service.

As I have said, the Church has a gallery over the entrance. Below this gallery is the font on the left hand side and there are also two rows of seats. This area was always reserved for the old squire who arrived just as the service commenced and who left at the commencement of the hymn sung immediately before the sermon. I cannot remember seeing anyone else seated in the area during a morning service even if the squire was not present. The seats on the right hand side were always occupied by the sexton and the bellringers.

Sir Fairfax Cartwright married a Roman Catholic lady so from that time the family did not worship in the Church, although they maintained a great interest in it.

As a boy I pumped the organ, there is still the space into which I squeezed and where I often found myself dozing off during the sermon. A little gauge consisting of a piece of string with a weight attached showed me when to pump harder, when the weight was up the bellows were empty, when the weight was down the bellows were full. I was hidden by a curtain but I often peeped round this where I could see (and be seen by) my father in his seat under the gallery.

As I have said I attended Sunday School, and each year (I think it was on the first Sunday but it may have been the first Sunday in Advent) we would be given a little book in which to stick the pictures and text we were given each week. There were spaces for fifty-five 'stamps' in these albums, one for each week and extra ones for Christmas Day, Good Friday and Ascension Day. The pictures were very beautifully coloured Biblical scenes and were much admired. Unless one had a very good reason for absence a stamp was given only for attendance at Sunday School, I had several full albums and much regret that I no longer have any of them, they would be treasured and I would dearly love to be able to show one to my great-grandchildren.

My father, who was a bell ringer, often told an amusing story of an 'extra terrestial being'. The occasion was the ringing in of the New Year, the bells were rung for some little while and prior to this there had been jollification and much drinking. One of the ringers, Oliver, found an urgent need to relieve himself of some of his intake of beer so went into the bushes near the church door. In the meantime, a new recruit to the team was approaching the church when, to his horror, he saw a white apparition. He fled through the porch and into the belfry where, almost collapsing he told of the 'ghost' he had just seen. My father was very concerned as the youth was terribly frightened and was almost hysterical. Suddenly Oliver returned, he was wearing a white mac and the 'ghost' was explained. It was some little while before the youth saw the funny side of this.

When I was about twelve I became a choir boy, although there were always twelve boys in the choir there was never any shortage of recruits, for one thing, it brought several little treats and privileges. Occasionally the choirboys were excused school in order to practise or to participate in a special occasion. Every year the rector, the Rev. W.D. Cartwright gave a Christmas Supper Party for the choir. There would be a plentiful supper and there would be crackers to pull which would reveal mottoes, jokes or quotations and tiny presents.

The mottoes and jokes were usually read out or the conundrums asked but one year my quotation seemed not something I wanted to read out, I quietly put it in my pocket and kept it for many, many years. I still remember the words so clearly, 'Paradise itself is insufficient for the discontented heart', would that some of today's generations could think on those words, I wonder how many people today would claim truthfully to be contented?

One year the choir had been taken for the day to the seaside, sadly it was before I was a chorister so I didn't go, I would have loved to have gone to the seaside, the sea was something one just conjured up in the imagination, in fact, I didn't see the sea until well into my twenties.

The church was heated by a boiler housed under the vestry. Every summer the coke for the boiler was tipped in a yard at the entrance to the church walk, this meant a two hundred yard trudge with wheelbarrows to the chute outside the vestry door a job usually done by the sexton but one winter he was ill so my father was asked to do the job of tending the boiler and I 'won' the job of wheeling the coke, I still remember the backache!

It would be true to say that after the Old Squire, who at that time was rarely seen except in church, the most important and influential man in the village was the Rector, Rev. W.D. Cartwright, he was the Squire's nephew and was universally liked and respected. He was a very just man and one to whom anyone in the village could turn for help and advice and be assured of a sympathetic hearing. After the death of the Old Squire in November 1915 the new Squire was Sir Fairfax Cartwright who was a semi-invalid and very rarely seen in the village. Lady Cartwright was a Catholic so the Rector's position in the village was somewhat different and, perhaps, less influential.

One incident concerning the Rev. Cartwright remains in my memory, it occurred when I was what is now known as a teenager. I was walking with two of the older gardeners when the Rector rode by us on his bicycle, neither of my companions acknowledged the Rector so I did not (although I did feel rather guilty about this). The Rector dismounted and called me over. Very quietly he said 'What would you have done had you not been with those men?' I replied that I would have touched my cap, to my surprise he smiled and said, 'Yes, I knew you would. I want you to remember that if you know in your heart that it is right to do a particular thing, then do it, no matter whose company you are in or what you might think they would say.' It was nearly thirty years later that the full force of his words came back to me. On Whitsunday 1945, there was to be a parade of the Home Guard in which I was Sergeant Major. The parade was cancelled as all Officers and N.C.O.s had to attend a demonstration at Company H.Q. so a parade was ordered for the evening. By this time the Home Guard had ceased to be a voluntary force and was subject to Army Rules and Regulations, an order given had to be obeyed so we attended the evening service. After the sermon the Rector, then the Rev. V. Banham, said that he would be celebrating Holy Communion after the service and that he hoped some of the men would attend. I remember I sat next to one of our officers (a farmer in civil life) who whispered that he would not be able to stay as he had another engagement. After the service the parade was dismissed and from then on the men were at liberty to please themselves so no one stayed for Communion except me. I walked out of the bright sunlight into what seemed like an empty church, it was not until the Rector took his place that I realised there were three ladies also in the church, I didn't want to be the only man so I turned to leave and walked to the porch, but suddenly the words of the late Rector came back to me 'If you know in your heart that it is right to do a particular thing, then do it . . .' So I returned to the church and took part in the service which had just begun. I shall never forget the sence of peace and contentment that I felt and which, thank God, I still have.

I used to put flowers and plants into the church for special occasions and festivals, however, this stopped towards the end of the War and Lady Cartwright being a Roman Catholic, the family involvement with the church decreased.

In a small rural community like Aynho one of the most important festivals of the church was at harvest time. Preparations started some weeks before the event, indeed, some villagers seemed to enter a competition which started months before to enable them to give of their best. The men would select onions and cabbage, beans, peas and carrots. The local bakers would make special loaves of sheaves of corn, the ladies would make special cakes, jams and jellies, marmalades and chutneys. The children would scour the hedgerows for wild flowers and grasses to decorate the church, huge sprays of autumn leaves would be gathered and altogether the church turned into a bower. Sadly the First World War saw the start of the decline. Quality gave way to quantity in the gardens and allotments and less could be spared to decorate the church, fewer flowers were grown but we children and young people still gathered the wild flowers, grasses, rushes and autumn berries combing the hedges and the water side for a goodly display. Of course, during Harvest Thanksgiving we sang the lovely harvest hymns, 'We plough the fields and scatter', and 'We give Thee thanks O Lord'. People from Aynho would travel to other villages to see the display and to take part in the services and other villages would come to us.

Now when I walk round the churchyard I see the names of many of my old playmates and of other people I remember so well. My parents are there, and the graves of some of the Cartwright family including the man I first knew as 'Master Richard' and who was both employer and friend. He is there with his only son, Edward, who died with him in a car accident in 1954.

Yes, the Aynho Church played a very great part in my life.

Chapter 5

To be a gardener's boy

And so I was thirteen, time to leave school and become 'a working man'. My first job, which lasted for three months was as a farmer's boy. This was not new work to me as I had often helped the farmer, during summer evenings and on Saturdays I had helped to drive cattle and sheep and done other minor tasks for which I had received a copper or two. Now I was employed full time, no forty hour weeks in those days. I worked from dawn to dusk and, in spare time often drove the sheep to neighbouring road-sides where they grazed, for this chore I received a few pence extra.

I had always spent most of my spare time around the farm as I had always loved horses and would often travel with the carter, I was sure the horses knew I loved them as they would always nuzzle me when I stroked them. The carters took enormous pride in their horses, grooming and caring for them, spending much of their own time on these chores. The horse brasses were polished and the leathers treated with various potions to keep them supple and shining.

The Aynho estate had two beautiful shire horses who would work without word of command. I was always impressed when I saw these lovely animals standing perfectly still whilst taking the strain of a tree being loaded on to a timber carriage. Horses are wonderfully intelligent animals, I have seen them walk from side to side up a very steep hill to enable them to take the heavy load to the top, this without any word of command from the carter.

Good carters, cowmen or shepherds were a very great asset on the farm, they dealt with minor ailments in their charges and prevented trouble for the animals in their care. Indeed, it was only on very rare occasions when an animal was seriously sick or injured that the vet was called. Many a wife has been heard to complain that her man thought more of his animals than he did of her!

I sometimes went with the shepherd and many of the sheep seemed to know me, especially the orphan lambs which I helped to feed using a baby bottle. I worked from 7.0am until 5.0pm, and for this received two shillings and sixpence a week (12½ pence in today's money). Not very much you may think, but skilled carters, cowmen and shepherds earned between twelve and fifteen shillings a week and general labourers only eleven shillings. Occasionally there might be 'perks', milk or eggs might sometimes be given to the men, sometimes a piece of pork or bacon and at sheep killing the head or even a small piece of mutton might be given. These days we seldom hear of mutton, it is always lamb now, but a good mutton stew gave very good and wholesome food for a family.

These workmen lived in tied cottages and loss of job meant loss of home, their lives were hard and the reward more for a job well done than financial. Farm workers were amongst the lowest paid workers in the land and in many parts of the country they suffered very great hardship with less than good employers. At Aynho we were considered lucky, we were treated very well indeed judged by the standards of those days.

This was not the case on many nearby estates. In one

village the gardener was sacked for admitting to having voted Liberal at a General Election. In another case, just the other side of Banbury, the head gardener was told by his employers, on the outbreak of the First World War, that he must volunteer for the employer's regiment. The man being no youngster and with a wife and family to support, declined to volunteer whereupon he was given instant dismissal and told to get out of his house immediately.

In both cases the employers perhaps did their men a good turn. The first man joined a local nursery and ended up owning it (with his son). The second man joined a very famous firm of seed merchants, stayed to become a famous and respected sweet pea expert, very much valued by his employers. But many men did not get other jobs and became more or less destitute.

Cases like these were quite common around the early part of the century, and indeed, before that. One can appreciate why the trade unions were able to proliferate and become quite powerful. They did good work in those days, but then they really did put the welfare of their members first.

Then, thanks to the intervention of the school master I was offered the chance to become the gardener's boy at Aynho Park House. I still remember the excitement with which I first entered those gardens as an employee, for the first time in my life I saw grapes, melons, peaches and nectarines growing in greenhouses. I still remember that the melons were just ripening. I cannot describe the distinctive smell but it remains with me yet. My astonished eyes were thrilled by the sight at the many plants, chrysanthemums and other flowers which were growing in pots all standing like rows of soldiers upright and smart, each one was tied and staked to wire supports. My childish eyes could not absorb all the new sights.

This was in July 1915, the First World War was raging, times were not normal and skilled labour was getting scarcer, so almost immediately after starting as gardener's boy I was asked to undertake work which would earlier have been quite out of the reach of a boy. To me this was a great opportunity and I accepted the challenge with great enthusiasm. In summer I worked from 6.0am until 6.0pm and in winter from 7.0am until 5.0pm from Monday through until Friday, on Saturday work finished at 4.0pm whilst Sunday was a day of rest, although attendance at church was considered obligatory. One was expected to be outside the gate ready to start work as soon as the gate was opened in the morning, even in the middle of winter, when it was still quite dark there was work which could be done. For example, manure could be wheeled on to vacant plots ready for use when the light was better, or ashes and clinker would be collected from the boiler house for disposal and new stocks of coke taken from the pile and wheeled about thirty yards to the 'stock-hole' for replenishing the boilers for the next twenty-four hours. Even in mid-winter evenings when it was really dark one was not allowed to leave before 5.0pm. You may think this a very long day for a child but it was work and work which I enjoyed, even better, I was paid for doing it, the princely sum of six shillings (30 pence) a week being handed to me every other Saturday.

Of course, I was just about the lowest of the low in the hierarchy of the gardens and I had little contact with the head gardener whom I called 'Sir'. The head gardener chose men to take charge of each section of the garden and allocated other staff to assist. I was put into the charge of the foreman of the glass department and was given responsibility for certain tasks. One of my major responsibilities was the care of the flower pots. All the empty pots had to be thoroughly cleaned before being put away, they all had to be stacked in their proper sizes and the first thing I had to do was to learn the various sizes and shapes. When asked for such and such a pot I must always fetch the correct one. It seems a small thing but there was quite a lot to learn. There were special shapes for various types of use, for example, there were shallow pots for orchid growing, these not only had drainage holes in the base but also around the sides of the pots. There were very special pots for seakale and rhubarb. These pots were like bell glasses with a lid with a knobbly handle and I still have one of these which I kept chiefly for sentimental reasons because one day, over fifty years ago I found my small son John, then aged three, planting his cousin in it. The cousin was on a visit from London and had been persuaded by John to stand in the upturned pot, when I arrived on the scene the pot was well filled with soil and John was busy firming the soil around his cousin by using one of my potting sticks. John had spent many hours watching me potting plants and apparently wanted to make his cousin grow. But I get ahead of myself.!

There were other tasks which were my special duty, each morning I must clean the boots of the head gardener, a job I did when I was sent to his house in the village to collect any letters which might have arrived. The second morning after starting work as garden boy I was told that after my midday break instead of going back to the garden, to report to the lady in charge of the laundry at the Park House. I had no idea why, or what I was to do although something was said about mangling, I thought this was rather strange on a Tuesday afternoon, usually Monday was the wash day. My surmise was correct it had nothing to do with mangling wet clothes but to operate a large press in order to press and smooth out all the creases on the dry and folded linen. When I entered the laundry I was amazed at the size of the room, the height of the ceiling, being as high as the width of the room; suspended from the ceiling were some wooden frames holding several lines so a large number of towels, sheets, etc could be hung up to dry when outside conditions made drying the clothes impossible. The wooden frames were raised and lowered by pulleys. Occupying nearly the length of one side of the room stood what looked to me like a long box made of polished wood, it was approximately four feet wide and two feet high. On the top of this box rested four wooden rollers, on which was another box the same width and height but not so long as the bottom box. In the centre of this box was a handle, it was this handle I had to turn so that the top box resting on the wooden rollers would move backward and forward. The items to be pressed were rolled on the first and last roller and when pressed to the satisfaction of the head laundry maid first one and then the other would be replaced by another supply of linen. This task took about three hours and when finished I would get a cup of tea and some cakes, needless to say I looked forward to Tuesday afternoons. Six months later with the death of the Old Squire and partial closure of the house these Tuesday visits ceased, also we were entering the third year of the First World War and I was wanted to do more important tasks in the greenhouses – I have no idea what happened to that old press, I suppose if found today it would be a museum piece.

Another of my tasks usually took one and a half days and was to lead the pony which was used with the mower on the pleasure lawns. I became very fond of this pony and would often steal away to the small paddock to feed him a little tit-bit. He was quick to recognise me as a friend and would come when I called him, he enjoyed the carrots, apples or knob of sugar which I usually had for him, sometimes the coachman could be persuaded to give me a handful of corn for him. I never had any trouble catching the pony when he was wanted for the mowing. He would always come as soon as I called much to the annoyance of the estate men who would often need him very early in the morning to pull the little light four-wheeled wagon in which they placed their tools and he often led them a fine old dance!

One job which I found very boring and tedious and I disliked intensely was the washing of the leaves of the large palm trees. The leaves were sponged regularly and I never did manage to gain any enthusiasm for the task. The two largest palms were used four times each year, at Easter, at Whitsun-tide, Harvest Festival and Christmas when they were used to decorate the church. One palm was placed each side of the altar as a background for the other plants and flowers. I was told the arrangements were traditional and had seldom been altered. At Easter and Whitsun pots of arum lilies were used with the palms and at Harvest and Christmas white chrysan-themums. The pots were hidden by specially grown plants of variegated euphymus and maidenhair fern. Other plants used were schizanthus and stocks, especially round the font. One type of stock much used was beautiful, it was of branching habit and had dark green leaves and pure white flowers and a scent which was strongly of cloves. This tradition of supplying the flowers to the church ceased in 1917 because of the shortage of labour and the need to concentrate on food production, the palms were destroyed and, much as I disliked having to sponge them, I was very sorry to see them go.

As more men were taken for the forces I had more contact with Mr Brown, the head gardener. I grew to admire and respect him almost as a second father. Beneath a somewhat stern and forbidding exterior there was a wise, kindly and understanding man. He was a patient man who would always find time to explain his theories to those willing to listen. I learned a great deal from him, much of which was to prove invaluable to me in the years to come.

There was a strict hierarchy in the gardens as, indeed, there was in the house. I remember an incident in my first winter working in the gardens. It was a Monday morning, I went to work and, to my great surprise, could find no one about. I went to the bothy where I was astonished to find the foreman and his second-in-command still in bed. I asked what my first task was to be and was curtly told to do what the hell I liked and to clear out as they were both leaving that morning. I reported to Mr Brown who gave me a list of tasks for the day, he told me to carry out these tasks to the best of my ability as many were jobs I had never done before. It seemed there had been a terrific row on the Sunday between Mr Brown and the foreman because, due to the neglect of the second-in-command the young shoots of the peach trees had been badly scorched which meant that both the crop of fruit for this year and the young shoots for next year's fruiting had been very badly affected. It appeared that there had been tension between the foreman and Mr Brown for some time, the foreman had been trying to discredit the head gardener and so get the opportunity to take his job, for a long time he had been working his way into the good graces of the young squire and the agent. He thought that if he could do something which could be blamed on Mr Brown his promotion would follow. Unfortunately for him, he lost his temper and told the young squire that unless Mr Brown left both he, the foreman, and his second-in-command would go. To his horror he was told that he could leave immediately. So now the two men were going. The bothy (gardener's house) would be closed and there would be just Mr Brown and me, the humble gardener's boy, with the help part-time of a good local gardener in the greenhouse.

There was another time when the tender shoots of the peaches were scorched. The paths in the greenhouses were of wooden slats, some had broken and were replaced with new ones. These had been creosoted to enhance their life. After the treatment the slats were left out in the open air for several weeks during the winter and then placed in the greenhouses. One warm day the paths and walls were hosed down to keep the temperature down but the water acted on the creosote and fumes rose, badly damaging the shoots. This occasion is firm in my memory as the paths were taken out again and I was given the task of scrubbing them with very hot water and soft soap until not the slightest smell of creosote could be detected.

It was about this time that, with several of my friends, I enlisted in the Local Defence Volunteers. We were under military age and were not allowed to bear arms, but we thought ourselves very important and felt our membership of this organisation added glamour to our image, especially with the girls!

Towards the end of the War, Mr Brown was able to engage a man who had been invalided out of the Army because of war wounds. Although this man did not intend to make gardening his career, nevertheless he was an extremely able and skilled gardener who excelled at growing plants under glass. He would grow certain species for a period of time until he was satisfied with the results achieved, then he would start growing another type of plant. One year he grew calceolarias and the next he specialised in zonal pelargoniums. I recall he once staged a display of these pelargoniums which was quite the finest I have ever seen. The following year he grew some wonderful cyclamen and gloxinias. When he lost interest in the plants he handed them over to my care, this was wonderful for me and I eagerly grasped the opportunity and challenge to care for the plants as he had done. I really tried to remember every little thing I had seen him doing in growing the plants, and often returned to the greenhouses in the evenings after my day was officially done. I learned much from this man and am eternally grateful to him.

This ex-soldier had moved into the bothy and invited me to join him, I realised that this would be a great help to me, especially as by this time I had realised that gardening was what I really wanted to do, that this was the career I wished to follow. I accepted the invitation to move and so went to live in the very gardens in which I worked.

I have mentioned peaches and nectarines several times, perhaps here I could talk about those fruits. Peaches are generally thought to have been recorded in China, around two thousand years ago before their introduction to the Greco-Roman world. Once again, as in the case of the apricot, Wolff, the monkist gardener to King Henry VIII may have planted the first peach tree in England. What a good thing for us that Henry was so fond of his food! Peaches and nectarines are of the same family, indeed, there are recorded instances of nectarines originating from the stone of a peach, and vice versa. Visually the main difference between the fruit is in the skin, the nectarine being smooth and the peach soft and furry. Until the middle of this century and with the exception of the grape no other fruit tree was so generally planted under glass as the peach.

In the British Isles outdoor peaches need the protection of a wall, in some warmer parts of the Kingdom they will succeed on a south or west aspect if the locality is not too elevated and exposed to cold winds. On the other hand, a low area subject to fogs and damp will prevent the wood from ripening and the trees are not a success. Without a doubt the best way to cultivate outdoors is a fan-trained tree against a wall. Planting needs great care. The ground should be well cultivated and sub-soil examined for moisture content before the trees are planted, trees will not flourish if the soil is shallow and resting on a dry or gravelly subsoil. These trees suffer very quickly from lack of moisture, exposed to the heat of the sun the leaves evaporate at an astonishing rate any moisture they have and, as long as the roots can supply this, all is well but as soon as the roots have exhausted the water supply the tree will quickly undergo a change for the worse. Even when the supply of water has ceased the evaporation will continue drawing from the juice of the tree; when this happens the red spider attacks the tree. This pest is difficult to eradicate but if neglected will destroy the tree completely within a year. It is useless to try to grow peaches on soil that dries out equally it is useless to plant them on soil which becomes waterlogged.

Fan-trained trees are best planted in October because peaches start early in growth. Trees should be planted about fifteen feet apart and I always found best results if the trees were put so that the main stem was some nine to twelve inches away from the wall but at an angle so that the branches were in close contact with the wall to gain the advantage on shelter and warmth. I always fixed a wire frame an inch or so from the wall, this gave me something on which to tie the branches and also provided air space between plant and wall. This method also helps to check the red spider, a real plague to fruit trees and which thrives on the warm dry surface of a wall. The name red spider is somewhat misleading, the pest is not a spider nor is it really red but in fact it is a brownish mite so small that it is difficult to see with the naked eye. Through a magnifier it can be seen as a roundish shape having eight legs. They cluster on the underside of the leaves and feed by sucking the sap leaving the foliage pale and sickly and liable to fall off. Dry conditions are loved by this nasty little pest so water is its greatest enemy.

Another trouble which may be encountered in the peach is

that cold will blister the leaves particularly when the cold follows a really warm spell. The growth of the midrib is arrested and the circulation of the sap obstructed, the leaves become swollen, inert masses. I have never heard of a cure for this so prevention is the best cure and this can be done by giving the leaves some covering, even a fine meshed net will help here.

Peaches fruit on one year old wood and no other, therefore it is necessary to ensure that year by year the entire tree is of new wood. Pruning is essential to successful cultivation and this should be done with great care. Consider starting with a young tree supplied by a good nurseryman, early in the season the buds begin to break throughout the entire length of each shoot. Some of these buds will produce leaves and others flowers. It is, of course, necessary to be able to distinguish between the types of bud, leaf buds are of a conical pointed shape and consist of scales surrounding the growing point. Flower buds are ovate and gradually become globe-shaped assuming a hoary appearance. The scales open and expose their downy external protective covering. Flower buds are much plumper than leaf buds.

Of course, one needs to see the fruit come to perfection but equally important is to ensure that a good supply of fresh wood develops to take the place of this season's fruiting wood. Because two-year-old wood never produces flowers it should not be allowed to develop. As soon as the fruit has been gathered much of the wood should be cut out. It would be wrong however to remove the entire shoot for it is set with wood which is going to produce the next year's fruit. The method employed is to pinch or rub out almost all the young shoots on fruiting wood during the season leaving only the two strongest at the base of each fruiting branch except that one should leave one shoot at the extremity to draw sap up past the fruit. It is then easy to cut away the fruited wood by cutting carefully just above the two young shoots which are left to provide next year's crop.

To summarise, during the growing season gradually pinch

out all the laterals from each piece of fruiting wood, saving only two at the base and the leader at the top. After fruiting cut out all the old wood, the cut being made far down the two basal shoots which are left to grow on, these are then tied in to take the place of the removed wood.

Young trees should not be allowed to carry more than a few fruit, on mature trees one fruit can be allowed to every square foot of tree surface. Thinning of fruit should be done very gradually.

Should any of my readers wish to cultivate their own trees as a bush they should first choose a sheltered spot facing south and they should begin with a maiden tree, this is a single one year old shoot with maybe a few laterals at the base. After planting, this shoot should be cut to a height of two or three feet then, in the spring strong buds will be seen. The branches which will break as a result will form the framework of the tree. After about three years all the pruning that will be necessary will consist of the removal of weak shoots or those which have carried blossom. Of course, the centre of the tree must be thinned to admit light and air. If the tree has its leading branches cut back it will prevent too tall a growth and mean strong shoots will break thus furnishing the tree with plenty of bearing wood. By the sixth year the head of the tree should be fully formed and bearing good fruit, it should have also reached the stage when all future pruning is confined to cutting back some of the shoots every year to induce enough young wood.

Protection should be given against frost, especially during the period between blossoming and setting of the fruit. Both peaches and nectarines are self-fertile but it is advisable to help things along by hand pollination during sunny spells. Just a few words about watering – one inch of rain is equal to approximately one hundred tons of water per acre. Three hundred pounds of water produces one pound of matter so a tree planted against a wall will be deprived of half the normal rainfall and additional watering may well be necessary. A peach border must NEVER be allowed to dry out, watering little and often is useless, when the slightest sign of dryness appears the whole area should receive a very thorough soaking.

At Aynho we grew peaches and nectarines under glass. These were all fan-trained, one of the lovely rewards for our work was the sight of the beautiful mass of pink which appeared each blossoming time. We experimented with six varieties of peach and four of nectarines. Our nectarines were Elruge, an excellent medium sized fruit which is a very old variety having been known before 1670, the name Elruge is believed to be an anagram of the name of the gardener who raised the variety during the reign of Charles II.

Then we grew a variety called Pineapple, a large fruit having a delicious flavour and, as its name implies, having a similar taste to a pineapple. This variety was raised by Mr Rivers but can be recommended only for growing outdoors in very warm localities.

Another nectarine was Humbolt, again raised by the famous Mr Rivers, it is a large tender, juicy fruit. Our other nectarine was Lord Napier, one of the best for both indoor and outdoor cultivation although again, outdoors only in warm locations. The skin of this fruit is rather thin and requires light shading under glass when ripening; Lord Napier was raised from the seed of Early Albert peach in 1869.

Our peaches also included several raised by Mr Rivers. Duke of York had large crimson coloured fruit and a most refreshing taste. Peregrine was first introduced in 1906 and is certainly one of the best and most handsome of peaches with very mellow and juicy flesh. This will grow outdoors in a sheltered position. Mr Rivers also introduced another variety which we grew, it had been raised in Waterloo, U.S.A. by a Mr Fish and was, inevitably, called Waterloo.

Two other varieties were Dymond, a first class tree excellent for outdoor culture with large fruit of good flavour and Bellergrade which we grew in the cold peach case.

I have mentioned the pest red spider but another, equally nasty, pest is leaf curl; this occurs when the plants are grown outside and is caused by a fungus which attacks the young leaves causing them to turn yellow, then red and distorted. The fungus also attacks the young growths which die back, the only cure is to pick off and burn all infected leaves and shoots. To destroy the fungus and to protect the trees a Bordeaux spray should be used, this at the end of February when the buds begin to swell.

I was always interested in the stone fruits and gave a great deal of my time to them, as I became more involved I learned to pack the fruit for show purposes or for market. Later, when I was a married man I often prepared a peach or nectarine as a treat for my wife – I would cut it in half (after peeling it) then add a spoonful of sugar in the stone cavity and fill it up with brandy, this would be set aside for an hour or so when the sugar would have dissolved and the brandy absorbed into the peach. I never did try it myself but my wife loved this fruit.

But once again I jump ahead of myself, perhaps now would be a good time to describe the gardens and tools of the trade which were to become such a huge part of my life.

Chapter 6

Tools of the trade

It was not until I went to work in the gardens that I realised just how many tools there were, or the importance of proper maintenance of them. Very quickly I was instructed that every tool must be cleaned and returned to its proper place after every time of use. Our tool shed was extremely well-equipped and arranged. There were brackets and hooks for all the sieves, ropes, scythes, rakes, hoes, spades, etc, there were drawers and cupboards for the small tools and clearly marked boxes for such items as labels, twine, pegs, nails and the other small impedimenta of a well organised garden shed. Wet days were turned to good use, tools were oiled and sharpened and any minor repairs attended to, it was well understood that more and better work could be achieved using clean, sharp tools than by those which were blunt, dirty or with rickety handles.

Many of the tools were completely unknown to me before I become a gardener's boy – tools such as the grubbing axe which was used to remove small trees. This tool had blades at each end, one was flat whilst the other was upright and could be used to loosen the soil and cut the roots of small trees 'grubbed out'. A drag was a small, three pronged implement

71

used instead of a hoe for loosening soil round vegetable crops. There were iron-headed rakes of many sizes, the heads being from four to fourteen inches wide; there were wooden rakes of various types, one had short, close teeth to take off the short grass from a lawn, this cleared the lawn so well that brushing was not necessary. The daisy rake had broad teeth which were sharp at both ends and was used to remove the flowers of daisies from the lawn.

There were several types of fork, one specially used for lifting potatoes had five flat prongs and was much lighter than the usual digging fork. Hoes there were in variety, one type for drawing furrows or drills, one for stirring up the soil, earthing potatoes and other crops. Men in those days were also inventive, my father made a splendid hoe from the blade of an old chaff cutter, the curved blade was some four inches by twelve and this was fixed by my father to a handle, it made very short work of earthing up potatoes, far less irksome than the usual hoe. A draw hoe had a blade attached to the socket by a slightly curved neck of solid metal whilst the Dutch hoe (or push-hoe) was used for cutting down weeds or for very shallow work on even surfaces. During the Second World War I bought a very useful second-hand tool, or perhaps it should be tools, this was a handle with a large number of accessories which could be adapted as drill, grubber, expanding drill, harrow, scarifier or ridging up tool, a very good buy, but, of course, that was much later in my career.

There were many kinds of scissor, each with its different use. Scissors used for thinning grapes had small tapering blunt points to avoid pricking the fruit, whilst the flower gatherer was constructed with two holes in one of the blades, this held the flowers as they were cut. I haven't seen one of these for very many years but it was very useful indeed when cutting flowers for the lovely arrangements for house or church. We had special scissors for cutting twine (although we usually used a knife) and many shapes and sizes all of which had their special use and place in the tool shed.

Of course, there were many, many knives of different sizes

and shapes, pruning knives, knives used when budding plants, knives with short stubby blades and knives with long slender blades. One with a very special use was the asparagus knife, this had a serrated steel blade with an iron shank fixed to a wooden handle, the blade would be pushed down the shoot to cut or saw it off near its base.

All items of equipment and tools were marked with the initials W.C.C. – William Cornwallis Cartwright. A branding iron had been made by the village blacksmith and hung on the wall of the tool shed, each new item was marked immediately it was received and even new hammer or tool shafts were branded when replacing old or broken ones.

The village blacksmith also made the nuts, bolts, staples and nails we used – we did not buy them in nasty little plastic packs which never have just the number you require. These small items were kept in the toolshed in their clearly marked boxes.

Mallets were made two, four or six inches in diameter and always from apple wood, a good wood for this purpose as it does not split and was always readily available. Whenever a large apple tree was felled some of its wood was left to season for subsequent manufacture into mallets. Of course, other apple wood was used for logs – it gives a lovely scent when burning.

Shears there were in plenty, different sizes for trimming different types of hedge, the shears used for fine topiary work were never used for cutting coarse hedges or trees. We had an old pair of sheep shearing clippers which gave very useful service when cutting grass close to a wall or round trees and bushes. These clippers were in one rounded piece and could be used with just one hand leaving the other hand free to remove the cut grasses.

One item in the toolshed which was forbidden to be used except in an emergency was a large hurricane lamp which was always filled with oil and ready for use. It hung on the wall and woe betide anyone who moved it unless it was absolutely necessary. There were oil lamps around the greenhouses and other carrying lamps available, but this particular one was the emergency lamp. I suppose such lamps would be museum pieces now.

There were many tools associated with the lawns. These included special turf cutting tools used when laying or repairing the lawn. Then there was the heavy cast iron roller. Every spring this roller was filled with water and its weight was then about one ton, it had shafts and could be drawn by a horse or a pony but was often drawn by three or four men, its motive power being decided by the state of the lawn, hob-nailed boots were very much forbidden on the lawns! The roller was emptied in the autumn before the hard frosts could freeze the water and burst the drum; besides the lawn it was used on the wide gravel paths, for narrow paths or those with intricate turns a smaller roller was used, this had its cylinder in two parts for ease of turning.

We had special long-bladed tools for removing suckers from roses and shrubs and for taking up deeply rooted weeds such as dock. I don't remember if these had special names nor do I remember a great deal about them as I have not seen one for more than fifty years and certainly I didn't have any during most of my time in the gardens, equally certainly they were there in my early days.

One truly formidable piece of equipment was the water barrel, ours held thirty gallons of water and was mounted on two large wheels. Over the years I have carted many thousands of gallons of water and very early learned the right and wrong way to manoeuvre this article, one should always pull the barrel, not push it. I learned this the hard way, one day I needed to move the barrel only a short distance so decided to push it, I hadn't noticed a stone in the path of one of the wheels, the stone stopped the wheel but the weight of the barrel swung it forward, the handle came up into the air catching me and removing a good inch of skin from the underside of my arm, a painful way of learning a lesson!

There were several different sizes of mowing machine, a small ten inch J.P. Minor was used on steep banks, I still have this particular machine and it still gives me good service. The twelve inch machine was pushed by one person but the fourteen inch was pushed by one whilst a second person pulled by means of a piece of rope. The thirty inch machine was horse or pony drawn, this had its grass box fixed on a moveable frame, a small wheel with handle was fixed to the right-hand handle of the machine and this connected via a chain to the box. When the grass box was full the handle would be turned lifting the box clear, it could be turned over and emptied and then, by reverse winding of the handle, returned into position.

Each craft or trade had its own tools. I often watched my grandfather sharpen saws. I remember he had a very large number of files of different sizes, each had a specific use for the various types of saw. He also had a saw-set, this was rather like a dinner knife in shape but the blade was thicker and stronger and had teeth of different sizes to correspond with the teeth on the various types of saw. With this saw-set the teeth were set to suit the type of wood to be cut, green wood needing flatter teeth than well-seasoned wood. My grandfather told me that after a saw had been used on a live tree it was essential that all juice and other adhesive substances should be cleaned immediately from the blade and the saw dried and oiled.

We grew willows for basket making and the willows were prepared with a tool called a stripping brake. This was a pincer-like tool with rounded claws which stripped the bark from the willow, the actual basket makers used a large variety of tools, knives with beaked blades, secateurs, shears and a cleave for splitting the willows. A grease horn was filled with tallow or grease to ensure that the bodkin ran easily through the willows. A flat bladed beating iron was used to hammer down the willows to ensure no gaps in the weave, a 'dog' was used to straighten the rods, this was a length of rounded metal with a looped handle at one end and two right-angled spurs at the other end.

The dry-stone waller used few tools, the main being his

hands and eyes, however a special hammer was used to chip off edges or protrusions to make a better fit of the stone. As I write this I have before me an old stone hammer used by my brother. It is about a foot long and at present it is without a handle. The hole for the handle divides the hammer into one third and two thirds. The smaller part ends in a rounded head whilst the longer end flattens out and curves into a blunt blade some inch and a half wide. My brother used this to build and repair the many miles of stone walls in and around the village and the Park House. In some instances templates were made to ensure eveness, these templates were usually legs of wood to the desired height. Of course, stone-walling is used all over the country and each area seems to have its own way of doing this, sometimes the top stones are cemented together but often nothing is used but the stone.

The blacksmith had a wide range of tools, the anvil being perhaps the most important although I suppose correctly, the anvil is not a tool but a piece of equipment. It always stood on an elm block near the hearth which was fanned by a large bellows. Our blacksmith was farrier as well as blacksmith so his range of tools was very large. For shoeing horses he used pincers to remove the old shoes, rasps to remove pieces of the hoof and a hammer to put on the shoes. I was interested to learn that there is only a small area of hoof which can be used for shoeing without pain to the horse. It always amazed me that the horses stood so quietly as if they knew that the farrier knew his job and would not hurt them, sometimes I saw all four feet shod in around half an hour. The blacksmith used many tools when doing blacksmithing, hammers of various sizes, wrenches, files, wire brushes, tongs for removing items from the fire, Fullers round-nosed tools which are used to draw hot metal in the required direction. Of course there was the water container into which the hot metal was dipped which was called a bosh. The blacksmith helped the wheel-wright when he made the cart wheels, it was the blacksmith who put on the iron tyre. The tyre would have been made to the correct size and then, when red hot, would be pushed on to the wheel which had been clamped to a stand known as a tyring platform. The blacksmith was one of the most skilled and useful members of the community. He made and repaired the tools other craftsmen used and without him work might have been even more difficult.

Mr Baughan was our wheelwright and he had a formidable array of tools. There were augers for boring holes, adze for cutting, calipers for measuring, spoke dogs and spoke shaves, spanners and mallets, compasses and chisels. There was a foot-driven lathe for wood turning and a special four-legged stand on which wheel sections are fitted. Many of the wheelwright's methods are those of centuries ago, the only difference being in the tools used, power-driven lathes now replace the old foot-operated ones.

The hedger and ditchers used few tools but their skills were enormous. They could 'lay' a hedge to make neat and secure means of preventing animals from straying. The tools they used were their hands and eyes with the aid of an axe, a slasher (for cutting away the undergrowth) and a billhook. The billhook had a shortish handle whilst the slasher was long handled. The other thing many hedgers used was a good strong pair of mitten type gloves as hands could be severely damaged in this work.

There were other trades which had special tools, the stonemason who used a variety of saws, gouges, chisels and mallets made of beechwood. There were still thatchers in my childhood in Aynho and they used large thatching needles for holding the reeds in place, thatching hooks which were driven into the rafters, eaves' hooks and shearing hooks to cut the reeds or straw whilst the materials were carried to the roof by means of a yoke. This latter was often just a two-branched piece of tree trunk with the two ends lashed to hold the reeds or straw.

These then were some of the tools used when I was young, but there was one tool used by many men for their personal toilet which was the cut-throat razor, a fearsome thing. A fine steel blade of some two or three inches was pivotted into a handle which protected the blade, the handle was about six inches long and was often made of bone. Sharpening these razors was an art, a leather strop was used, this was perhaps two inches wide and about eighteen inches long with a moulded leather handle at one end and a loop at the other. It would be hooked over a door handle, coat hook or similar, the handle would be held at an angle of about forty-five degrees then the razor would be pushed up and down the leather. A flick of the wrist at the end of each stroke would ensure that both sides of the razor were sharpened. An oil stone was also used occasionally to ensure a truly awesome cutting edge. Many men had several razors, indeed, many had one for each day of the week and would make quite a ritual of sharpening all the razors often doing this on Saturday afternoon or Sunday morning. When I was young many men were bearded and beards were clipped and neatened by use of scissors. But then came the safety razor and the electric razor and the old cut-throat was relegated, indeed, many ended up being used for such mundane tasks as would normally entail the use of a pen knife – I even knew one old man who said the cut-throat was ideal for trimming off the corns from his feet!

Of course, the farm equipment was different to today's mechanical marvels. There were no combine harvesters, the ground was ploughed by using a horse-drawn plough with a man driving the horses and taking great pride in his straight and tidy farrows. Seed was sown by hand although a form of horse-drawn box seeder was being used in some areas, the resultant crops were cut by a horse-drawn cutter of revolving blades although some were still cut by hand. Crops were stacked (or stooked) by human endeavour after men, women and children had tossed and turned the corn or hay by using wooden rakes or long-pronged forks.

All this was slower and more labour intensive than modern methods but I wonder if the present day mechanical ways are so much better? One thing I can be sure of, the only 'pollution' from the old methods was provided by the horses, and that was a very useful additive to the soil!

Chapter 7

Aynho Park House gardens

The area immediately around the house was known as the pleasure gardens, a term usually used in those days. The gardens always reflected the tastes of the owner, some would be formal, some informal, some would be left as parkland right to the house. At the beginning of my association with the gardens they were both simple and formal, they complimented the house and its design.

As I have said, the house had been rebuilt after the Civil War, the central three-storey part had been rebuilt by John Cartwright but between 1707 and 1710 there had been extensive additions made for Thomas Cartwright, the style of these suggests that the architect might have been Thomas Archer a man who was also Groom-Porter to the Court of Queen Anne. The existing buildings had been extended to the west to form a library, to the east to form a conservatory or orangery. The house was re-faced giving it the appearance it has today and wings were built flanking the courtyard on the north side.

Prior to Archer's remodelling the entrance was on the south front but he transferred it to the north when he created the courtyard. In the middle of each wing there is a framed window which, more than anything else proclaims Archer's hand in the remodelling of Aynho. Under each window is a lettered slab which was taken from the pier at Cherbourg by Thomas Desequillieres whose daughter married into the Cartwright family.

In the period 1800 to 1802 Sir John Soane was employed to remodel the interior of the house increasing the height of the Archer extensions and adding an attractive arched structure between the wings and the main block. Since that time Aynho Park House has known various changes to suit the taste of successive owners. The structure of the house and the collections it used to contain reflected part of the Cartwright family and made the lovely building a home.

Perhaps whilst I am mentioning early Cartwrights I could tell of William Ralph Cartwright who was born in 1771 and was the only son of Thomas Cartwright. During the Napoleonic invasion scare William Cartwright was largely responsible for raising the Brackley Volunteers. He also represented the County of Northamptonshire as its Member of Parliament for forty-eight years. Indeed, the Cartwright family wielded so much influence during the eighteenth and nineteenth centuries that this part of the country was often called 'Cartwright Corner'.

It was during the tenure of William Cornwallis Cartwright, grandson of William Cartwright, that in 1915 I had joined my father and grandfather as employees of the Aynho Estate and the Cartwright family.

I was fascinated by the gardens and quickly learned my way around them and learnt the special features. The gardens complimented the house and so, on the south the formal beds were set out. There were thirteen forming a large circle which was divided into quarters by two gravel paths. Within this circle were other circles each of four beds, again, all being separated by a narrow gravel path. All the beds had edgings of neatly clipped box. In the centre was a final bed in the centre of which stood a large stone urn. In summer months this bed

81

and the urn were always planted with a wonderful display of ivy leaf geraniums. The second circle of beds was planted with calceolarias and the third circle with heliotrope the outer circle again with geraniums. Over a thousand plants were required for this display and these were specially grown in pots. It was a near military operation to plant these beds for the job had to be completed in one day. I, as garden boy, would join five men in this task. One man would remove the old plants, two would follow digging and manuring the beds. My job was to turn the plants out of the pots ready for the other two men to plant them in the freshly prepared beds. I only participated twice in this task as the summer of 1917 was the last year in which they were planted in this elaborate way. They were neglected for a while then re-stocked, then, during the Second World War the box became unsightly and there was no labour to care for the beds so Mr Cartwright decided that they should all be swept away. A simple design was substituted of eight beds in a new hedge but this was not until well after the War had ended and the army, which had occupied part of the grounds, had gone away.

Not far away from these beds was another planted with rhododendrons, this was surprising as there was too much lime in the natural soil for these plants to grow successfully so the whole bed must have been specially prepared many years before. I guess this was done during mid-1800s as when I joined the staff, in 1915, the rhododendrons were already some ten to fifteen feet in diameter.

On a large lawn nearby, there were six large circular beds of standard roses which were interplanted with dwarf bushes of the same variety – in later years this bed was planted with the rose General MacArthur.

Along the terrace in front of the house were six large agaves, sometimes called the century plant. The leaves of this plant are very thick and stiff and end with a sharp spike. The flowers are a yellowish-green or red in colour and are borne on spikes from one to forty feet in height depending on the age – they seldom flower before they are ten years old and grow on for sixty years or more. Our Aynho plants were about ten feet in height and grew in boxes two-and-a-half feet square. On the day before the Annual Flower Show I had the unenviable task of fixing a cork to each of the spikes to a height of six feet from the ground. Putting these plants into their winter quarters was a truly hazardous operation. These agaves and the rhododendrons were swept away after the First World War.

To the south-west of the house is a large triangular area which was known as the Wilderness, so called because, except for a few winding paths it was covered with trees and shrubs. To the south-west corner was a yew walk planted at the time of the Restoration, this was on a huge mound which I always understood to be the site of a Cavalier burial ground. The yew walk terminated in a semi-circular shape protected by a low wall which had been erected to prevent the unwary or reckless from falling thirty feet to the park below. In later years a small platform was built behind this wall and the site used for clay pigeon shooting. The competitions were exciting and difficult as the competitors were way below in the parkland. Originally this area had been known as The Bastion but in my day it was known as The Mount. During the Civil War it had been part of a line of fortifications to which the house was attached by means of a drawbridge.

The large amount of soil which had been excavated to form The Bastion had left a large basin; from my earliest days in the gardens I had wanted to see this cleared of trees and undergrowth and made into a miniature lake but to my sorrow this was never done.

To the west side of the Pleasure Gardens there was another such basin some twenty-five feet in diameter and about fifteen feet deep, its steep sides were covered with ivy and I never did discover if this was a natural basin or how or why it had been made but it made an ideal dumping place for leaves, lawn mowings, etc. Except in very dry summers water always stood in the bottom; during the next twenty to thirty years the continuous use of it as a dump gradually filled the hole until it was as if it had never existed. To the south-west was another such pit but this had an arched doorway much of which was under water. Again this was used as a tip and eventually filled in but I wonder if it was part of an older house or church from centuries ago? I suppose I will never know the answer to that question.

There was a lovely old summer house at the end of a path at the top of the Wilderness. This house was of very unusual design and shape, it was open for half its circumference but not as is customary to the south, but to the west because of the lovely background of trees and shrubs. This old house was completely smashed in a dreadful storm in 1947 when an old elm crashed down on it. After the clearing up operation the whole of the Wilderness was cleared just leaving the yews, the site of the summer house was now open to the sun. I would have liked to have salvaged everything possible and to have re-built the house using much of the same material. For example, the floor was of pebbles with a central design picked out using the knuckle joints of deer killed in the Park. The roof was made of hundreds of small cones gathered from the estate whilst another design in the floor used larger cones. The walls had been osier shoots whilst estate rushes had been used to pad the inside walls and make a seat, I loved that old house and was bitterly upset when it was destroyed. I never did like the structure which was put in its place, a domed roof supported on six columns resting on a raised floor in the centre of which stands an ancient Saxon water vessel which was one of a pair unearthed by a ploughman in a field just north of the village.

To the west of the summer house was a lovely, fine old English rose garden, planted originally in the year 1700. There were some magnificent trees in the gardens and park and I will write about those later. Another feature of the gardens was the ice house, this was utilitarian, not decorative. It was built in 1818 some two hundred yards from the house and was in the shape of an egg some fifteen feet in diameter and twenty feet in depth. In the floor was a deeper hole filled with bricks and stones to allow drainage. Most of this structure lies below ground level, the excavated soil being piled on top making it resemble a giant molehill. The mound was planted with laurel bushes and spring bulbs and with the limes nearby ensured coolness and shadiness for the ice-house. After the coming of refrigerators the ice house was no longer required so the laurels were grubbed out and the mound turned into a delightful rockery. Access to the ice house was by way of a passage built into the north side of the mound, this led to a thick, heavy oak door built into the north side. Then came another passage six feet high and five feet wide ending in still another door which opened into the actual ice house. Of course, only one door was allowed to be opened at a time.

The ice house must have been invaluable in those early days before we all had refrigerators. When there had been a severe spell of cold weather the tenants would provide horses and carts and would convey the ice to the ice-house. This ice would be cut from the canal and nearby ponds, it would be cut in convenient-sized pieces and some poor chilly people had the job of building up the ice into walls as each load was delivered, it was levelled and lined with straw. This task was the honour of the gardener's boy and I was that boy on the last occasion that the ice-house was filled, little did I think then that many years later I would have the great thrill of showing the ice house to millions of people through the medium of a television programme, indeed, who had ever dreamed of television in those days?

The nearby lime avenue was generally thought to be one of the finest in the country. The trees were planted about twenty-five feet apart with banks of laurels a few feet behind them. The base of each tree was allowed to bush out and then clipped to a ball. Facing the Park was the Sunny Walk. Being sheltered from the north and overlooking the parkland this walk was warm, even in winter. There were garden seats at intervals and in spring it was beautiful with hundreds of bulbs flowering gaily. This was one of the favourite walks of the Cartwright family and especially of the Old Squire who, weather permitting, would walk along there every day accompanied by the Head Gardener, Mr Brown. On these occasions no other workman was allowed in the vicinity to intrude on the Squire's privacy. A bridle path led from the main road to the village of Souldern. This passed under the lime avenue making a tunnel which was a favourite meeting place on Sunday afternoons not only for the Aynho boys but also those from Souldern. Many a game of pitch and toss was played in that tunnel. Evergreen oaks had been specially imported from France and planted to hide this bridle path.

The desire for upper-class privacy was very strong in those days, so, in front of the house was a large circular area flanked by the drive and planted with tall evergreens such as holly, laurel, bay and yew. These trees almost completely hid the house from view from the road, just the very uppermost part being visible.

Along the side of the Sunny Walk was a ha-ha. This feature was not uncommon on estates and consisted of a wall sunk where the pleasure grounds meet the parkland. It is inconspicuous from the house and gardens and behind the wall is a ditch on the parkland side. The purpose of the ha-ha is to stop cattle intruding into the pleasure grounds. Of course, this type of boundary provides uninterrupted views across the parkland from house or grounds. Aynho's ha-ha is nearly five hundred yards in length and varies in depth from seven to eight feet, the parkside of the ditch opens out to become a sloping bank whose crest is slightly lower than the level of the lawn, the slope blending into the parkland which slopes gently away from the house and pleasure gardens.

The park was divided into sections by belts of trees or iron fences whilst a trout stream flowed through from east to west and on into the Oxford Canal at which point a barrier was supposed to stop the trout from escaping. After heavy or persistent rain many a local fisherman would try his luck below the barrier in the hope of catching a trout which had escaped over the barrier and many a family enjoyed a fine trout caught this way.

(TOP) North face of Aynho Park House as seen from the road, c. 1924.
(ABOVE) Part of the pleasure grounds, also photographed in 1924.

(ABOVE) Outside staff, local tradesmen and others at the twenty-first birthday celebrations in July 1924 for Mr Richard Cartwright who is in the front row, wearing white shoes. Others include in the front row second left, Ted's Uncle Tom then Jimmy Dunn the carter from Souldern, Ted's father, Mr Westbury the head gamekeeper, Mr Brown the head gardener is on the other side of Mr Cartwright, then George Page the stonemason, Teddy Mobbs the blacksmith and Mr Meadows the head woodman. In the second row, Mr Maxwell the lawyer is far left with Mr Wightman the estate agent next to him. Fourth is would-be fireman George Butler, then Ted and his Brother Joe, then Cousin Harry.

(BELOW) South and East faces of the Church showing part of the Norman tower.

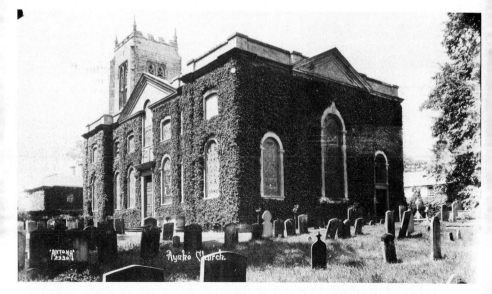

(ABOVE RIGHT) 'Aynho for Deddington' (Great Western Railway).
(ABOVE LEFT) The stocks as they were when Ted played around them as a boy.
(TOP) Ted's old home as it is today.

(RIGHT) May Day 1913, Bertha Clements, May Queen Gertie Garrett and Joan Clements.

(BELOW) Gertie Garrett crowning her 1985 successor — the village's last May Queen.

(ABOVE) Ted's wedding group, 21 April, 1925. From the left, Mrs. Freda Skipworth the mother of the bride, bride's cousin 'Rene', Ted, Zarita, Brother Joe, second bridesmaid, and bride's father, Frederick Skipworth (every inch the superior butler!)

(BELOW) Wedding group when sister Ethel married Arthur Cooper. The bride's parents are on the left, Joe is behind the bridegroom, Sister Florrie is the bridesmaid whilst Ted's parents are on the right.

(ABOVE) Apricot picking. Joe's wife is on the ladder and the boy is Ted's nephew.

(BELOW) Aynho Park Fire Brigade circa 1930. First left in front row Ted's father (with his famous moustache), next to him Uncle Tom. Brother Joe and Cousin Harry are in second row second and third from right.

(TOP) Ted with Cattleya Portia during the late 1930s.
(ABOVE LEFT) The old water cart being pushed by Ted outside the old (1880s) bothy.
(ABOVE RIGHT) The entrance to the ice house.

(ABOVE) Ted and Percy Thrower in the BBC Birmingham studios in 1960.

(BELOW RIGHT) Hippeastrums with white daffodils, one of two groups in the dining room as part of the Easter decorations.

(BELOW LEFT) Zarita and Ted in one of the greenhouses. Picture taken by Mrs Cartwright when celebrating Ted's fifty years of service.

A herd of deer roamed the parkland – they had been there for very many years long before the first Cartwrights took up residence. The size of the herd was controlled by shooting some of the bucks each year. It was a lovely sight to see the herd grazing or resting beneath the trees at the top of the park. One of the favourite places was below some walnut trees, it seems flies do not like walnut trees so the deer knew they could have an untroubled graze or rest in the walnut shade. In spite of the considerable barrier made by the ha-ha deer would jump the barrier in search of food when snow was on the ground, I have seen many deer leap the barrier and many a young shrub or the rose bushes suffered as a result. I never found it in my heart to blame the deer for their damage to the trees. Efforts were made to ensure that they had sufficient food to make these forays unnecessary. Often I would creep quietly from shrub to shrub and then lie perfectly still watching these beautiful animals from a distance of just a few yards.

It was a sad time for me during the Second World War when the Army occupied parts of the park and many of the deer became very wild and began roaming through the broken fences into the surrounding countryside. The majority would return to the park but many did not, causing damage to crops and danger on the roads, especially after dark with vehicles allowed only very little light. It was decided that the herd must be destroyed; by now I was Head Gardener and loved the deer. I made a plea that a small part of the herd should be preserved suggesting that a small enclosure could be made with the ha-ha forming one side, expert advisers considered that even this would not contain even a small herd determined to roam, so, regrettably the idea had to be abandoned and the herd was destroyed, so ending a tradition which had lasted for many centuries. However, some deer had escaped and even now there are still a few roaming the surrounding countryside and I get great pleasure from the thought that they are descendants of deer which lived on Aynho estate from the days of the Normans, or before. During the 1973 harvest a local farmer told me of two deer bounding out when he began reaping a field of corn.

After the deer had been destroyed the park never seemed the same again – something was always missing. Now many of the beautiful trees of the parkland have gone and the park is agricultural land. Looking out from the Park House it seems strange to see corn growing where once the deer roamed. In the winter there is brown earth instead of green grass and it is only when snow is on the ground that the park looks as it did in those days when I was a boy.

Chapter 8

Aynho trees

I have mentioned, in passing, many trees but I would like to tell you more about the beautiful specimens which I grew to love in my years at Aynho Park House.

The estate and park were blessed with many magnificent trees, somehow even the common countryside trees seemed to take on an aura when seen in the park. I think of all the rare and beautiful trees in the gardens and one of my favourites was a magnificent Ginkgo Biloba or Maidenhair tree which, it was believed, had been presented in the early nineteenth century to General Cartwright by the Honourable Charles Greville, one of the founders of the Royal Horticultural Society. Another fine specimen was of the Cedar of Lebanon (*Cedrus libani*). The oldest cedar in this country is reputed to be one planted as a seed by Dr Edward Pocock in 1646. It is believed that Dr Pocock brought the seed back from Lebanon and planted the tree in the grounds of the old rectory at Childrey near Wantage in Oxfordshire. In 1970 it had attained a girth of over twenty-five feet.

I have already mentioned the lime trees in the Lime Avenue but one thing I must mention here. In the 1920s a large area of evergreen laurels, box, etc had been grubbed out from near the Lime Avenue and the area cleaned levelled and sown with grass seed, but before the grass was sown thousands of bulbs had been planted, daffodils and bluebells. Every year from then on until the Second World War at daffodil time the grounds were open to the public on what became known as 'Daffodil Sunday'. A band would be employed to play and people would walk along the Lime Avenue enjoying the music and the flowers.

In the park evergreen oaks (or Holm oaks) were planted to hide the footpath. This is one of the finest evergreen trees capable of being grown in this country. It is a truly noble tree with an abundance of foliage. The young leaves are covered with a whitish down which soon falls away leaving the upper surface a beautiful dark, glossy green. Perhaps the one defect of this tree is that it sheds its old leaves in May and June, this is a time when dead leaves are really not wanted in the gardens and grounds but the pleasure given by the sight of this lovely tree outweighs this minor defect. The oak stands pruning and clipping and is a truly beautiful tree when carefully trimmed and shaped.

Another tree I must mention is one that stood in the pleasure gardens, it is a specimen Catalpa (Bignoniaceae) or Indian Bean Tree. This is a hardy deciduous flowering tree with large attractive leaves. The flowers are very beautiful and remind one of small gloxinias – the flowers are white, bell-shaped with yellow and purple colour within the flowers which are produced in abundance in July and August.

At the beginning of this century Aynho estate was practically self-supporting having its own stone, sand, gravel and clay pits but one of the chief blessings was the vast number of forest trees such as oak, ash, beech, chestnut, elm, hornbeam, lime, walnut (which gave us walnuts at Christmas) sycamore, larch, etc. Larch was an extremely valuable timber, important economically. It was used for a hundred and one jobs including re-roofing cottages. Oak and elm were also economically valuable, their timber was also used for many jobs although re-roofing was not one.

One of the major uses for elm in the old days was to provide the wood for pumps. In those days most cottages had their own well with its own pump. The wood for the pump piece would be bored out with an auger, great care being taken to ensure no movement of the timber during this operation, this was ensured by strategically placed trestles supporting the wood. The auger was a fearsome tool, of necessity it was six to seven feet long with a handle some three feet long, this length was necessary as it often took two or three men to turn the handle. After the holes had been bored in the sides of the bottom pump piece it was lowered into position with the aid of a 'pit roll'. This latter was a pole about six feet in length which had a length of rope wound round it. A metal level was attached to either end and after the rope was secured to the bottom end of the pump piece it was lowered into the well by men operating the levers. The base of the central bore would be plugged to prevent any mud at the bed of the well from polluting the water supply. In addition, the side bores were protected by a series of nails or wire netting to prevent loose debris, frogs or toads from blocking the supply of water to the main channel. My grandfather, father and brother were employed in making these pumps. Footholds were made in the sides of the well to enable a man to descend to carry out any necessary work or repair. The wells were usually about four feet in diameter so, as a precaution, anyone descending was always secured by a rope. Most of the wells had been made many years before using local stone in its rough natural state and they were usually thirty to fifty feet deep.

My father once told me that the first and most important task in well and pump work was the selection of the straight young trees to supply the timber. Only elm was used for pieces below ground level, the elm selected being taken, if possible, from the hedgerows, the wood being tougher than that from trees growing in the woods. The trunk would need to be at least ten feet long, twelve to fifteen inches in diameter. Obviously, for some deep wells several pieces of timber had to be used, the shafts would be tapered gradually and then fitted into the next piece which had been gouged out to take the tapered shaft. To make both ends watertight they were smeared with a linseed oil putty and then joined by an iron band. This procedure was continued until the last shaft had reached a point just below ground level. On this piece was fitted the last, familiar top section which would have been constructed out of oak. A great deal of time and ingenuity was expanded in providing good water supply to a home; today's generations, used to hot and cold on the turn of a tap, can have little or no conception of the labour involved in getting one's water to drink, wash but not waste.

Trees for pumps and wells were felled and used immediately while in their green state but the top section was usually of wood that had been felled some three or four years before use, and allowed to season. Elm was always used for below ground work because it is the one wood which is almost indestructable when in constant water. It is when wood is first wet then dry that it quickly rots and although many sections of the pump were not in constant water they were, nevertheless, in a permanently damp and airless place and anything but elm would last a very short time.

At the beginning of the century wood was cut using a saw pit and a cross cut saw but this gave way to a steam engine driving a circular saw. The first such implements we had were out in the open but eventually the engine and saw were housed in a different part of the grounds under cover, this made life more pleasant for the men using them. During the First World War thousands of trees were cut down especially larch and spruce, which, after being stripped of bark and cut into suitable lengths were taken to the Aynho railway yard for loading and subsequent usage as pit props or for dug-out props in France. Other of our timber was used for duck boards in the trenches on the battlefields of France and Belgium. Much of this work was carried on twenty-four hours a day as the war dragged on and more and more props were needed, this decimated parts of the estate and, after the end of the war, a large part of the old kitchen garden was laid out as a nursery for all kinds of forest trees which were subsequently used to re-stock the woodlands.

Every year there was a wood sale in December and dealers came from all over the country to buy the oak, beech, ash and walnut. Apart from those sold at the December timber sale few mature ash were ever cut down. Ash used on the estate for gate posts, rails, etc was taken from specially grown trees planted in several acres known as the 'ash-beds'. A limited number of trees in one area would be cut down each year to eighteen inches above ground level, the stumps would then send up two or three shoots in the first year, then these would produce three or four stumps which would in turn grow more. All would be allowed to grow on until they reached the height of some eight feet when they would be thinned out to one strong growth on each stump which would grow on to fifteen or twenty feet and with a diameter of six to eight inches. All this would take approximately ten years. The thinned out wood was used for bean sticks, broom handles and such like.

The beech was valuable for its timber but also for its very attractive appearance. Some, for ornamental use, were grown as specimen trees, others in a small cluster and either way the trees were beautiful, the copper beech being particularly attractive for decorative use. Occasionally a mature tree would have to be felled, only the trunk would go to the timber yard for use or sale, the branches, or leg wood as we call it, would be cut into logs for the fires in the house where it was considered a very safe timber for logs. When dry it burnt well and never threw out sparks. The bushy boughs would be tied in bundles and sold as faggots whilst the nice, straight, twiggy pieces would be bound on to a nut or ash pole and used to make a besom brush to be used for sweeping paths and lawns of leaves.

Perhaps I might digress a moment. The big house did not have central heating and, in winter, could be cold and draughty. In the evening, when the lights were lit and the curtains drawn, mattresses would be carried into the rooms and placed behind the curtains to help stop draughts and to keep the rooms warm. Of course the rooms became stuffy, but stuffiness in small quantities was considered better than cold and draughts. Often the stuffiness would become too much for the ladies who would retire early!

As well as elm's utilitarian role in pumps it was frequently used for making outside furniture. Its wavy grains helped to make attractive tables, benches and seats and the mellow grey to which it aged was both attractive and in keeping with its surroundings.

There were several clusters of elm in the village, one of which was particularly a favourite with the young members of the village. It was planted on a steep bank which had been part of the fortifications during the Civil War, parts of this wall still remain visible amongst the roots. It was into these roots and the worn-away butts of these very old trees that we would creep and hide singing ribald songs at the passers by. The two elderly spinsters who lived opposite were frequently targets:

> Lillian Dunn sat in the sun
> She burnt her bum and away she run
>
> Lou, look at me looking at you
> Lou, look at your damned great shoe.

Oak was grown extensively, the native English oak is one of the longest living trees. Its wood is of great value being very durable so suitable for such uses as floors, doors and general house building. In olden days it was much sought after as a wood for panelling. It is, perhaps, the real 'King of the Trees'.

The acorns from our oaks were gathered and ground into a meal which was used to supplement the diet of pigs. Only a small amount was included into the pig food but it was a valuable addition. We children used to make a few extra coppers gathering the acorns and selling them to the farmers or pig rearers. Of course May 29 was celebrated as Oak Apple Day, and we would search for the acorn cups to wear as favours or, if the cup was intact with acorn, to 'smoke' as pretend pipes.

We also had Spanish oaks which are inferior in quality of timber to the English oaks but are hardy, quick growing and of elegant habit.

Perhaps the most stately trees on the estate were the Wellingtonias in the park. An old gardener told me that Wellingtonias were planted at Blenheim Park and pointing in the direction of Aynho, whilst those at Aynho pointed to Blenheim. It was very sad when, in 1959 two of the Wellingtonias near to the house had to be felled, they were dying from the inside, a large hole being found in the trunks although there had been no sign of decay around the outside of the butt.

There was a cluster of three walnut trees at the bottom of the garden and one large walnut tree which stood near the 'bothy', as soon as it shed its fruit the nuts were gathered and stored in sand to keep the kernels plump and fresh for Christmas. If any did shrivel they were allowed to steep in milk and water overnight.

I have already written of the larch trees, which were always regarded as really tough but I remember the only time I ever saw one which had been blown down in a gale. This was in 1947 on a Saturday afternoon. The men had gone from work when I heard a dreadful crash. On investigating I found a very old larch had crashed across the road completely blocking it. This was a main road so something had to be done and quickly too. With the help of Father and Uncle Tom and a cross-cut saw we cut the tree into sizes which enabled them to be moved by a horse and tackle. The road was quickly open to traffic and another job, of clearing up the pieces, ready there for Monday morning.

Care was taken in selecting trees to be felled, especially in the park. Immediately one was felled two would be planted in its place, the strongest one would subsequently be allowed to stay and grow. The local blacksmith made little wire cages for putting round the trees to prevent damage by the deer and cattle. I well remember one morning when I saw the head gamekeeper hurrying through the garden, he had a gun and I asked him what he was going to do (it not being the shooting season) he told me that a deer had been trapped by its horns in one of these iron cages around a tree and he was unable to release it so would 'put it out of its misery' by shooting it. I was upset about this and asked if we could not together have a further attempt to release the animal but he was adamant that it was kinder to kill it. He explained that this particular deer was leader, or king of the herd so the other bucks would quickly attack it, if they had not already done so. Sadly I had to agree that it was kinder to kill it.

My father being a woodman of considerable skill and knowledge I was early at home in the woodlands around the village and in the parkland. I often went with my father on Saturday mornings and during school holidays and from him learnt a great deal of forest lore. I remember I once asked him why hornless deer would be at one end of the park whilst those with horns were at the other end, thus I learned to tell the difference between does and bucks.

There were some fine specimens of chestnut trees in the park and several clusters of them around the estate. As deer

are very fond of chestnuts – both 'conkers' and sweet chestnuts – we children did not do too well in our search for the desirable fruits. However, there were two trees which certainly supplied us well. These were in the garden of the Rectory and one was the largest chestnut tree I have ever seen. But our favourite chestnut tree was the one in the centre of the village green at the lower end of the village. Not only did this supply us with our annual supply of conkers but also gave us a playground, both under and in its branches.

My love of trees developed at an early age and it has never gone. Now, when I visit the village I look for those old, beloved landmarks and friends, and sadly I sometimes look in vain.

Chapter 9

Between the wars

I have mentioned Mr Brown the head gardener, a man for whom I grew to have very great respect and affection. As this man had so much influence on my life perhaps I should tell you something about him.

During the latter part of the nineteenth century a firm called Veitches were nurserymen who also kept a register of skilled gardeners who were seeking jobs. Veitches were 'choosy' about the people they recommended, they had a reputation for supplying good men and this they were not prepared to lose. A young man called Brown was working for Veitches and was put on their register as he wanted to go out into the world as a head gardener. A post was notified to Veitches and Brown was recommended and accepted; the job was to start in about a month. Imagine his disappointment when a further letter was received saying that the former gardener had been reinstated, a cheque for a month's salary was enclosed and a hope that the young Mr Brown would quickly find another post.

Realising his bitter disappointment, Veitches wisely advised Brown to write to the gentleman thanking him for the cheque and asking for a recommendation should there be another post in the neighbourhood. Three months later a further letter was received from the gentleman suggesting that Mr Brown should write to Mr Hibbert of Aynho Park, Northamptonshire. In those days it was only the head of any branch of staff who was appointed by the lady or gentleman of the house, each head employing his staff.

Mr Hibbert was a tenant of Aynho Park House grounds and gardens having taken it on a seven year lease during the absence of the owner William Cornwallis Cartwright. And so, the man to whom I was to owe so much became head gardener, a post he held until I took over from him many years later.

Mr Hibbert was not an easy man for whom to work but he early recognised the worth of Mr Brown and, on his moving from Aynho, he asked Mr Brown to move with him. This the head gardener did although he was sad at leaving the many friends he and his wife had made in the village so it was with great pleasure that he received a letter from the Rev. F.C. Cartwright asking if he would like to return and take up the post of gardener to Mr W.C. Cartwright, he delightedly accepted.

It was customary for the gardening (and other) accounts to be on the desk of the owner by 9.0am on the first Monday of a month and this led Mr Brown to tell me of an amusing incident which befell his brother-in-law who was head gardener of an estate in Ireland. He often employed an old Irish labourer who, in turn, would submit his account for the month. On this particular morning he arrived late and the account had to be presented before checking. The owner was a lady who, when she reached this account suddenly broke into a peal of laughter. Looking over her shoulder the gardener saw, with horror, 'Manure £2.0.0d; Carting leaves £1.10.0d; Buggering about 5/-.'

When Mr Brown was with Veitches they showed a plant at the Royal Horticultural Society Show, this was the Golden Rayed Lily of Japan (*Lilium auratum*) which gained an Award of Merit. I believe that this was the first time *Lilium auratum* had been seen in London. The precious plant had been taken across London in a horse drawn vehicle supported between the knees of the man in charge. This story, told to me by Mr Brown, enthused me and I felt that one day I too would show at the Royal Horticultural Society Show and that I too would grow a *Lilium auratum*. I did both, but not for a long time after. Some forty years after I was told this story I grew what I felt was a fine specimen. Growing in an eight inch pot it grew to a height of nearly seven feet carrying twenty-three perfect blooms, all of which averaged six inches in diameter, I still have a picture of this plant towering above me as I stand beside it.

So we settled down after the end of hostilities. As I have said, Mr Brown had employed an ex-soldier and I was sharing the bothy with him. A good bothy was considered a great asset and the availability of such a dwelling featured prominently in advertisements in the situations vacant columns of the *Gardeners' Chronicle*. An advertisement might read 'Journeyman required, large gardens with. . . feet of glass, good bothy available for right applicant'. I remember the amusement with which, some fifty years ago I read such an advertisement which ended 'no long-haired poets need apply'. A journeyman was one whose status was between a gardener's boy and foreman. In some larger establishments there might be first, second, third and even fourth journeyman in each department.

Our bothy at Aynho was splendid. Often the bothy was just a room or two over the store or potting shed but, towards the end of the last century Mr Brown had persuaded the old squire to build a new and modern bothy. It was a bungalow with spacious rooms and separate bedrooms. It was furnished from the servants' quarters at the house, indeed an additional advantage of living in the bothy was that the occupants were recognised as indoor staff and, as such were invited to attend functions in the Servants' Hall. This also gave the advantage that indoor staff were appointed on a monthly basis whilst outdoor staff were on a weekly appointment.

One of the women, usually the wife of an under gardener, was employed to do the housework in the bothy and to cook our mid-day meal. Of course, on Sunday we had to fend for ourselves but sometimes the cook would take pity on us and give us a Sunday dinner. Each Saturday morning I drew cleaning materials which we needed from Mr Brown who, with Mrs Brown, inspected the bothy once a month looking at everything, including the linen.

We were allowed free fruit, vegetables and milk from the Home Farm and occasionally a couple of rabbits or a joint of venison came our way from the gamekeepers. Having all this largesse meant that our purchases from the village store were small. I kept the accounts which we cleared each fortnight when we got our pay, I remember we usually had to pay about eleven shillings each. Not much you may think, but then, my wages were only about twelve shillings a week. Alternate weeks we were on duty which meant that from midday on Saturday until the same time the next week we were responsible for the gardens, particularly the greenhouses and, furthermore, were not allowed to leave the gardens during that week. For this I received an extra five shillings on my weeks of duty. You were always on call. Perhaps a job needed doing in the house, the gardener expected to find you in the gardens or bothy at any hour of the day or night during your tour of duty.

Often I was called out to start the fires in the stoke holes when it was found that the temperatures in the greenhouses had become too low. It was impossible to shirk one's duty even if one had wanted to for the small indicator needles would register the minimum and maximum temperatures reached during the night.

After the war these regulations were gradually relaxed, the imposition of maintaining an exact and unvarying temperature in the greenhouses were discontinued and provided one's allotted duties were performed correctly it was no longer necessary to remain within the garden precincts after normal working hours.

After I had been living in the bothy for some months the ex-soldier asked if his wife could join him so I had to return home to live with my parents who, during the war, had had three soldiers billetted on them. These soldiers were generally known as 'hay balers' a troop of soldiers similar to the Pioneers of the Second World War. Many of these men helped on the farm and some on the estate. One even stayed on after the war and became the estate lorry driver, he married a local girl and later became chauffeur to Sir Fairfax and Lady Cartwright.

After the war men began to return to the estate, some were crippled, one, a member of the kitchen staff returned having lost both legs. It was in the spring of 1919 that the ex-soldier decided to leave which left Mr Brown, myself and a young village lad to carry on as best we could until a suitable new man could be found.

Again, I was lucky. The new man, who came to us from the estate of Sir Ernest Cassell was an exceptionally skilled gardener, especially working under glass. He was a single man and suggested I move back to the bothy to share with him, which I was delighted to do. During the next twelve months I was gradually expected to accept more and more responsibility, even for jobs which, before the war I would have been barred from even helping with. I learnt quickly and easily remembered what I was taught. Perhaps this was because I did not have the same host of teenage problems which seem to beset youth today. My new foreman was a splendid man and I got on extremely well with him. He was a confirmed bachelor and was able to devote a great deal of time to helping me with my studies. During the late autumn of 1920 there must have been some trauma at the house for, for reasons not disclosed, the bothy was closed, there was a further reduction of staff when my foreman left and so, at the age of nineteen, I was asked to take charge of the greenhouses with just the help of a young boy.

My old foreman moved to Woburn Abbey and I often went over there to see how he was faring, indeed, also to continue to learn from him. He was living in a most palatial bothy. The living quarters were one side of the drive whilst the sleeping quarters were situated on the opposite side alongside the potting sheds. At that time every type of fruit was grown at Woburn – Muscat grapes, melons, stone fruit and all manner of plants.

These periodic visits to Woburn afforded me golden opportunities to learn to grow plants some of which I had not even known existed. The knowledge I gained there from my old colleague remained with me and was extremely beneficial when I eventually became head gardener at Aynho and was in a position to choose for myself what I wanted to grow.

July 1924 saw the coming of age of Richard, only son of Sir Fairfax and Lady Cartwright. This was indeed an auspicious occasion and was celebrated in the lavish and extravagant manner of the time. There were parties and dinners for guests at the house whilst all the villagers and estate workers were invited to parties and celebrations.

For some time I had been courting a girl from the neighbouring village of Charlton-cum-Newbottle. She had the lovely name of Zarita but was usually called Rita. I had met her at a dance and then again at another dance on the lower lawn of Charlton Lodge the house at which her father was butler. We always went to the flower shows of the other villages around and it was at the dance after the Charlton Show that I met Zarita again. It was a very romantic setting with terraced lawns and beds of flowers on the one side and the lake with coloured fairy lights on the other. If I close my eyes I can still see a large swan of fairy lights reflected down on to the waters of the lake. I believe that this, and for me an auspicious occasion, was the last time the flower show was held at Charlton on such a grand scale. There followed a period of casual friendship and mild courtship but then we drifted apart. I was invited to Zarita's twenty-first birthday party which was held at the Cottage, the country home of the Earl of Birkenhead, to whom her mother was cook-housekeeper. Of course, the Birkenhead family were away on this occasion, *noblesse oblige* really did not include actually being present at the birthday party of one's housekeeper's daughter, indeed, the house was usually only visited by the Birkenheads at weekends. Little did I know at that time that this house would become nearly as familiar to me as was Aynho Park. The party was not a great success for me, for one thing, Rita was being courted by a Charlton boy and had little time for me. About two years later that romance broke and Rita was forced by ill health to give up her job as school teacher. Her ill health was due to a particularly bad attack of peritonitus when she was about sixteen which left her with various weaknesses.

I was still very fond of her and, at the suggestion of a friend, decided to go to see her and we resumed our old relationship. Her father rather objected and this could have been only because of my class. I had a good permanent job, and a good, reasonably modern home available should I desire to marry. They could have had no real objection to me personally, I neither smoked, drank nor gambled. I saved my money and led a blameless life; so the objection could only be on class. Even then, the class consciousness of servants was greater than that of the employers. We have all heard of 'upstairs downstairs', but there was also a hierarchy of 'inside, outside'. Although on the surface this made little difference to our personal relationship, nevertheless it made me very conscious of my social standing especially as Rita's sister had married the personal chauffeur to the Countess of Kimberley. This determined me that one day, in some way, I would make a name for myself, own my own house, and be someone of whom I and our families could be proud.

So, in the spring of 1925 Rita and I decided to marry. I asked Mr Brown if the bothy could be re-opened to be my home. Sir Fairfax and Lady Cartwright gladly gave their consent so the carpenters and decorators were called in and the bothy quickly made into a very pleasant home. On the 21st day of April 1925 I married my Zarita. Lord Birkenhead loaned his Rolls-Royce for the occasion to take Zarita to and both of us from the beautiful old church at Newbottle. It was fitting that I should marry there as, with Newbottle Manor, the Church had been part of the Aynho estate. On my wedding day I determined that one day, when I was able to raise my own seedlings, I would name a new plant after my wife. I was able to fulfil the dream, first with a hippeastrum and later with an orchid.

My wife did not always enjoy particularly good health, due, so the doctor said, to the illness she had earlier had, indeed, he told her she was lucky to be alive. However, we soon settled down to a happy life. We were both fond of dancing and, during our courtship, had cycled many miles to a dance which would probably start at 8.0pm and finish around 2.00am. This would mean that after taking her home and then riding back to Aynho I was often abroad at three or four in the morning.

I remember one such occasion when it was a very dark night and I was riding through a wooded area and a sheep 'baa-ed' the other side of the hedge. I nearly fell off my bike. I literally jumped from my saddle and was only saved from falling to the ground by the cross bar. On another occasion in the same stretch of road I was startled when a large shape zoomed down on me; it was getting dark on a late summer evening and the shape scared me until I recognized it as a large owl which dropped down from one of the trees and flew about a yard above my head until I cleared the trees. Perhaps it is incidents like this that gave rise to many of the old folk stories about ghosts, certainly I am not afraid to admit the thought crossed my mind on both these ocassions.

I was always conscious of Rita's home and standard of living, so different to my own at Aynho, the son of an estate worker was much lower than the daughter of a butler, and her sister was lady's maid to the Hon. Mrs Greville!

Rita and I soon settled down to village life. There were entertainments such as cricket matches and tennis, in the summer with football matches and practising for concerts and musical evenings in the winter. Musical evenings were very popular, many homes boasted a piano and parties would be given at which there would be cards played, music made and good food eaten. So much more pleasant than the rush and bustle of today.

Visits to Banbury were also made. There was just one bus operating between Aynho and the town, which ran on Thursday and Saturday (market days). It left Aynho at 2.0pm and returned from Banbury at 4.30 but on Saturday there was a further bus which left the village at 5.30 and returned at 10.15, this allowed us to visit the cinema which was just becoming popular. Many is the time we have rushed from the cinema to get the bus, still thinking of the *Perils of Pauline*, or the trials and tribulations of Lilian Gish.

It was inconvenient to have to use the bus so I bought a motor-cycle. I used to take my wife to Banbury in my dinner time on Thursday, giving her more time for her shopping before she came back on the bus at 4.30. I was able to take my wife to visit her friends and relations often leaving her there whilst I returned to work in my spare time, concentrating on plants in which I had special interest. There was no such thing as paid overtime in those days except for grape thinning, a task which we carried out in very early morning or late evening.

In 1928 Sir Fairfax Cartwright died in London, his body was brought home to Aynho and placed in the church on the day before the funeral. A guard of honour was formed from men working on the estate who kept watch over the coffin until the funeral service. My brother and I performed that sad duty between the hours of 2.0 am and 4.0 am. It was eerie in the church, there was just one small light by the coffin and I was glad I was not alone, the silence indeed seemed the silence of the dead and my brother and I spoke only in whispers. I don't know why we did this but I do know that the chiming of the clock at 3.0 am made us both jump with fright.

The estate passed to the only son Richard. The death duties which were levied on the death of Sir Fairfax were drastically heavy and economies had to be made, both in the house and in the gardens. At this time, Mr Brown the head gardener, having attained the age of seventy years decided to retire. I was surprised, delighted and a little scared when Mr Cartwright invited me to become head gardener in place of Mr Brown and to operate with a reduced staff. For the first time we were required to sell all surplus produce to supplement the upkeep of the gardens.

The new squire (whom we had known as Master Richard) still retained his rooms in the Grammar House where he lived with his mother. During this time he formed a village cricket team from the village and estate. We had fixtures with many of the surrounding villages but the one fixture which always created great enthusiasm was the annual match with the Northamptonshire County Police. Our matches were played in the area known as Rylands Hill. The Lime Avenue had originally been intended as the grand entrance to the house and passed through this field providing a marvellously picturesque setting for our cricket. The field was regularly plagued with moles who ruined the playing area with their burrowing and to end this nuisance we planted a large expanse of half-inch wire netting beneath the turf forming the pitch. Mr Cartwright was also president of the fire brigade and arranged an annual party which was held each New Year's Eve. Each fire brigade member was invited with a lady companion, in addition the president invited many others and my wife and I were always delighted to get an invitation. On the day before the party we would transform the fire station with flowers and evergreens making it very festive. This event increased in popularity, other brigades being invited until it all became too big for the fire station and had to be transferred to the village hall just a few yards away. All the men of the Aynho estate had to take part in fire drill. There was one exception, however, a man whose eyesight was very defective and who was considered more of a liability than an asset. He was bitterly disappointed at this decision and resented it greatly. If there was a fire outside normal working hours he was always one of the first on the scene, the fire in Borton's farmyard was no exception. But by now the Aynho Brigade was part of the national fire service and no unauthorised person was allowed near the fire. This man still felt he was being badly treated and insisted on being there getting in everyone's way until a very well directed jet in the middle of his back knocked him face downward into a pool of filthy black water. He was absolutely soaked and beat a hasty retreat – much to the amusement of onlookers. It was after the outbreak of the Second World War that the fire brigade was incorporated into the national fire service and was controlled by the County Council. The Aynho engine was commandeered and taken over by a unit at nearby Deddington, and so another tradition had come to an end.

In 1932 the squire began to entertain again in the Park House and later that year he married Elspeth, only daughter of Lord and Lady Weir. So the newly married couple moved into the Park House, together with their servants and we were back in business. Extra plants were required, particularly large specimen plants for the house decoration. Two large glass houses were reconnected to the hot water system and once again I had the task of building up a collection of plants suitable for decorating a large and beautiful home. In the following chapter, I will describe the greenhouses and my work in them.

Chapter 10

Aynho greenhouses and kitchen gardens

At Aynho during the 1800s there was a lean-to greenhouse just over forty feet long which vaguely resembled a deep frame sunk into the ground. It had a nine inch flue built into the walls and was heated to the level required to grow pineapples. It was, in those days and even afterwards, referred to as 'The Old Pine House'. Towards the end of the century this building was converted into a span-roofed house and was used chiefly for growing melons. Instead of the old heating system using hot air a boiler and hot water system was installed using the same chimney stack. The old path became a larger reserve water tank, whilst the flue pipe from the boiler just under the eaves on the north side returned to the boiler via the water tank so utilising all possible heat.

After a very heavy spell of rain the smaller water tanks in the other greenhouses became full so, to prevent valuable rain water going to waste (and all plants prefer rain water to tap water), the surplus was carted by means of a two-wheeled water tank and tipped into the large reserve tank. I am sure this saving of water must have helped in producing our fine fruit and blooms.

Long before I started working in the gardens the green-houses had been extended and the heating supplied by three boilers in three separate stoke-holes. This heating had been changed in the late 'eighties from the previous system in which two large boilers had been connected to one very large stoke-hole. This stoke-hole was quite an interesting building. It was a lean-to affair some twenty-five feet long, fifteen feet wide and twelve feet high above ground level. Inside the ground had been excavated to a depth of ten feet and given a brick floor on which stood the two boilers. These were fearsome devices, one a seven sectional boiler and the other an old saddle-back type which was actually used only as a reserve. A flight of steps led down to this floor for human access but for the coke a cavity had been made about three feet up the wall with an opening to the path above. This cavity, which had an arched roof, was capable of holding about two tons of coke. As gardener's boy one of my tasks was to see that there was always a good stock of fuel in the cavity.

The change-over from three separate stoke-holes to just one was carried out during the absence abroad of the Old Squire, William Cornwallis Cartwright. It was a very expensive mistake. Prior to this, in the event of a breakdown in any one stoke-hole, there were two others to carry on the essential heating task, with only one hole one would be left at the mercy of the weather until repairs could be effected. Another big financial advantage was that one, two or three boilers could be used as required, in mild spring or autumn two were often shut down so conserving fuel. With only one it was heat going to waste. Indeed, with only one stoke-hole heat often went where it was positively not wanted and could not be turned off. The difference in the fuel bill after the change was so great that the head gardener who had been responsible for the change-over was dismissed. It was after this dismissal that Mr Brown was asked to return to Aynho.

The coke was bought during the summer months; sixty tons

were ordered each year, if the winter was really severe then even this huge amount might not be enough! It arrived at Aynho Station, at the rate of either a five or eight tons every week. My mind boggles at the thought of the cost of this fuel today! In those days, however, and bought in those quantities a ton of coke cost very little compared to today's prices. Indeed, I believe that even in the days when I was head gardener the coke was only about fifteen to eighteen shillings (seventy-five to ninety pence) a ton.

One of the more boring and tiring of my gardener's boy tasks was to remove the clinkers and ashes from the floor of the stoke-hole and sieve them using an inch sieve – any pieces of unburnt coke were returned to the fuel stock for re-use. A good stoker was an asset to a garden, by nursing the boiler he could probably save the equal of his wages for his employer. For instance, a good stoker would know exactly when to shut down the boilers to maintain the required temperatures. He would ensure that ashes were removed from under the fire bar and not allowed to accumulate blocking the flow of cool air to the fire. Blockage by ashes could cause the fire-bars to corrode and burn through very quickly.

Great care had to be taken to ensure ventilation in the stoke hole, care was also needed when large clinkers were being removed as they emitted sulphurous fumes. We were lucky, we had a large stoke-hole with plenty of air vents which allowed the fumes to escape quite quickly, even so, I have often had to escape up the steps with great speed, gasping for breath. Some large gardens did not boast an open stoke-hole, some had potting sheds built over them, or storage sheds and more than one unfortunate stoker or gardener succumbed to the poisonous fumes before he could reach fresh air, of course, such places would not be tolerated now.

The boilers I have described supplied only the greenhouses, the Park House was heated from a stoke-hole built on to the side of the house, there was a ten sectional boiler and the only opening was the door. It was a very narrow building with storage for only about two hundredweight of fuel, the only descent to the boiler being by means of an upright ladder fixed to the wall. Keeping the stock of fuel available for stoking this boiler was a very long term task.

Of course, had I been a gardener's boy a century or two before I would not have had even the refinement of a boiler. I was told that the Oxford Botanic Gardens used an apparatus which was a four-wheeled wagon filled with burning charcoal and this was drawn backwards and forwards along the greenhouse paths by a gardener. This method was used certainly until 1675. If a conservatory or greenhouse was built as a lean-to on a south wall there would be a good shelter for plants with the sun warming it by day and radiated heat at night but in very cold weather the poor gardener would be employed all night in wheeling his burning charcoal wagon. This method of heating gave way to subterranean heat conveyed by a stove built underneath the conservatory or greenhouse.

There were various methods tried to heat both house and growing areas. In the early days of gas fuel there were various systems which conveyed heat along pipes from a furnace and then back to a chimney, many of these were not completely successful giving off unpleasant, not to say dangerous, fumes. The dry heat and fumes resulted in the demise of many greenhouse plants and, when used in a house, gave rise to some unpleasant effects for the human occupants.

As I have said, during a period of retrenchment I was put in charge of the greenhouses even though still a very young man. I was so lucky that this should happen as I had fast become interested, almost addicted, to greenhouse culture. Going further back though, I still recall the thrill, awe and excitement I felt on my first visits to the greenhouses when I looked towards the roof and saw strawberries ripening in winter, when I smelt the strange and exotic scent of ripening melons, peaches, nectarines, grapes and figs, when I saw the strange and beautiful flowering plants the like of which I had never seen before. To be given charge of this empire at nineteen would have been beyond my dreams back in 1915 when, as a boy of not quite fourteen, I was first allowed to peep at the wonders.

At Aynho we grew grapes for the house. They were a frequently used fruit, no dessert dish being considered complete without a bunch of beautiful, freshly cut grapes, and we supplied between two and three hundred bunches over a period of around six months of each year. I was taught both pot and free culture.

We always used the very best loam to plant our vines, first in a six inch pot and then in one larger until finally it would be in one at least twelve inches in diameter. We used loam of a type very difficult to obtain today, and very expensive but it is possible to make similar loam, if you are willing to take time and trouble. Just leave the lawn edging for about a year. If this is against a cement or stone path you will have an edging some two inches wide with a mass of fibrous roots. These roots should be chopped up and to each bucketfull add a tea cup of bonemeal, a little charcoal or wood ash, some well rotted manure (making sure it is free from worms, especially wire-worms). Our two vineries were of lean-to construction against a stone wall fifteen feet high and which was eighteen inches wide. There were also, in the same area, two large span-roofed plant houses which faced east-west, a long, brick built frame with removable lights, a mushroom house and the forcing and storage sheds. In the same part of the grounds was the kitchen garden which was divided into four by grass paths three feet wide (during the Second World War these paths were dug up and used for potting purposes). Of the four parts of the garden one was used for fruit – we grew gooseberries, raspberries and the various currants. Another part of the garden was used for vegetables of which we had to supply top quality produce to the house all the year round. Until 1947 when it was destroyed in a gale, there was a cold peach house. Of course, there was a large number of frames each some six feet by eight feet and having removable lights.

When I joined the staff there were many men working in this area, some of them sons and grandsons of men who had

113

worked in those same gardens, these men all had great pride in their jobs and were skilled at many different aspects of garden work. Indeed, I remember one man who had been employed there for more than fifty years who told me that his father had also had more than fifty years' service. Another memory I have is of the man who scythed the lawns, he made them as level and smooth as any modern lawnmower.

By the time I joined the gardening staff ways had been devised of regulating the heat to the various greenhouses and this enabled us to provide fruit for very long periods of time. Indeed by planting outdoor fruit in different aspects we were able to prolong fruiting seasons of these fruits as well. We planted plums on both the east and west walls and so were able to pick fruit from July to October. We also planted Morello cherries, gooseberries and currants against a north wall and so ensured a late crop. Another advantage of planting such fruit against a wall was the ease of netting and so preventing the deprivation by our feathered friends.

In the vegetable gardens we had the usual vegetables, we first grew early potatoes and then maincrop and the same for peas, beans, celery and so on. There were thirteen beds of asparagus, each was twenty-two yards by five feet across. By stopping the cutting of shoots showing some six inches above the ground at the beginning of June, instead of the more usual later part of the month, we were able to cut a bunch or two of prime asparagus right up until late August.

We also grew sixty clumps of rhubarb. Twenty crowns would be lifted for forcing and to provide twenty strong crowns for planting in a previously prepared bed. The next twenty crowns would be gently forced by covering the crowns with rhubarb pots (bell-shaped pots with a top opening of about six inches in diameter) the whole having been covered to a depth of two feet with leaves and long strawy-manure. The third twenty crowns were left to develop naturally and this gave a long fruiting period.

We carried out much the same system with strawberries. We had eighteen rows each twenty-two yards long. The first six rows would not be allowed to fruit but would supply the new strong plant runners which would grow in pots to start a new bed in the autumn. Some of these pots were used for forcing in the greenhouse and we always expected to have ripe strawberries for Easter. The second six rows, which would be in their second year, having been the previous year's first six, would give large, succulent prize fruit for dessert, the final six rows being third year plants, would provide fruit for preserving.

Of course, this area also contained an orchard. This was sheltered from east winds by a beautiful wind-break of beech trees. We grew many varieties of fruit – damsons, mulberries, quince and medlars as well as the usual apples, pears, plums, cherries, greengages and so on. I well remember a Blenheim Orange apple tree which stood over thirty feet tall. We grew some apples and pears in the inner, more sheltered garden too, especially such dessert varieties as Cox's Orange Pippin and the Doyenne du Comice pear. I mentioned our medlar tree, this is a peculiar fruit, not much grown now. The fruit is quite unsuitable for dessert purposes until it begins to decay.

It is a sad thought that today, where these lovely and productive gardens once were there now exist luxury bungalows!

It was in 1917 that a big change took place. Lady Cartwright was very fond of flowers and it was decreed that there should be less forcing of fruit and vegetables but more pot plants would be grown. Then, as the war progressed there were further economies. We were reduced to just the head gardener, myself and a still younger boy (remember, I was only about sixteen or seventeen myself!) so the vines were cut out in the two large vineries and other economies made. It was at this time, when I was being asked to undertake work which, just a year or two earlier would have been declared far beyond my province, that Mr Brown wryly remarked to me that, in London, a man sweeping leaves or dog droppings in a small garden would be called a gardener. He made very sure I fully deserved my own title and claim to it, ensuring that I was well versed in all aspects of my chosen profession.

So when, at nineteen, I was asked to take charge of the greenhouses I responded to the challenge, first for my own pride I suppose, but even more, because of the respect in which I held my boss and tutor. At this time I was a reasonably good and very keen cricketer and footballer but I realised that these hobbies would have to go, the greenhouses would be a very full time job, seven days a week. I had no real hesitation, the opportunity was too good to be missed. I told Mr Brown that I accepted with two conditions. One was that I had a free hand to grow what I wanted, the other was that he would tell me if he saw I was doing something wrong. He readily agreed!

By now economies had meant that only a few of the greenhouses were heated so my first priority was to decide what to keep and what to dispose of. I devoted most of my spare time to working in the greenhouses, often working late into the night by the light of a lantern. The knowledge I gained stood me in very good stead when, in February 1928 Sir Fairfax Cartwright died, and Mr Brown, who by then was seventy, decided to retire and I was asked to take charge. I had one man to help in the kitchen garden and a boy to help me in the greenhouses. Gone were the days when the head gardener had a huge team of men with a foreman for every department and a team of journeymen and boys for each foreman. I was told to keep expenses as low as possible and to sell such surplus as I could.

Of course, my salary was increased and I also earned an extra bonus of one shilling in the pound for everything I sold. However, much as this extra income was welcomed, the greatest and most important aspect was that I was given a completely free hand to grow whatever I wanted and thought would be most profitable. This also meant that for the first time, I could fulfil my ambition to raise plants from my own selected seed. Later, too, I was able to grow orchids but more of that later. My old friend and mentor, Mr Brown, took a very great interest in everything I did and it is a great sorrow to me that he died before my greatest triumphs of which I will tell later. However, he did see and admire the beautiful orchid Cattleya Portia, which I had increased from ten blooms to nearly one hundred.

During this period after the death of Sir Fairfax Cartwright the Young Squire, Mr Richard Cartwright, lived with his mother in the Grammar House and I continued to grow some of the plants which had been the pride and joy of the old head gardener. I can still remember the special chrysanthemums which Mr Brown grew, this was a plant in whose culture he really excelled and his prize blooms, growing in rows in the autumn, attracted many visitors and won for him very many awards at the Banbury and Oxford Chrysanthemums Shows. In those days these shows were very popular and it was a point of honour that all the big gardens around would send exhibits. I remember one occasion when I was sent with a message to Charlton Lodge Garden. Of course I had to walk both ways and when I returned I was questioned very closely on what I had seen, what plants were being grown and the quality of the blooms.

To grow the large blooms and specimen plants special treatment was afforded the plants. Final potting always included three top dressings of rich compost, usually described as 'solid feed'. These dressings were done at intervals the intervening period being used for 'liquid feeds'. The liquid feeds would be started about a fortnight after a 'solid feed' and would take the form of a weak manure and soot water made by standing a bag of soot in a container of water. The soot would be old, fresh soot was left to stand for several months. Other liquid feeds contained sheep or deer droppings. Another feed was administered every other week, a teaspoonful of Epsom Salts being added to a gallon of water. This same solution was used during the evening to spray on both sides of the leaves. When a plant was watered it meant filling the pot to the brim, during very hot weather I would walk between the rows spraying over the pots with a watering can with a 'rose' attached.

During the late summer or early autumn, before the plants

117

were put for wintering in the old vinery, we would hold the pots balanced on a box and tipping the plants downward over a bath they would be thoroughly syringed with a solution called 'No-pest' which was both fungicide and insecticide. We would spray a dozen or so plants then drain the solution which had collected in the bath, this was done using a very fine sieve when the solution was used again.

Another group of plants we grew in quantities was geraniums. We often staged a display of over a hundred pots grown specially for effect. Cuttings would be taken each autumn and inserted into a small pot, one to each pot. In early spring these cuttings, having rooted, would be transferred to larger pots and stopped (having the growing point removed) for the first time. This would be continued, planting into larger pots each time until they were in eight inch pots when they were placed outside on a bed of ashes. No flowers were allowed to develop during this time until the later part of the summer when eight to ten buds would be allowed to grow on. In the middle of September the plants would be cleaned and their pots scrubbed and taken indoors to stand on shelves covered with moss. The moss was kept damp to make the correct atmospheric conditions until the colours started to show on the blooms when they were taken to the display area.

In the two span-roofed houses which faced east-west there were a great many plants of many varieties. In the warmest house grew palms, ferns and many beautifully coloured foliage plants such as caladiums the leaves of which were blotched or veined red, pink of white. Crotons were grown in a variety of form and colour and dracaenas with their richly coloured leaves. Rex begonias were another favourite and the fibrous rooting begonia, Gloire de Lorraine, which, with its graceful habit and wealth of flowers made it an extremely rewarding plant to grow. In the early days we had just two orchids – one pot of Coelogyne Cristata which was white with a yellow base to its lip and two pots of Cypripedium insigne.

In the cooler house were many cyclamen, other begonias, gloxinias and hippeastrum. Such flowers as stocks were also grown, partly for their wonderful scent and in the cooler part of the house was a large camellia, growing in a tub two feet high. It was trained to resemble a large ball and hours were spent sponging its leaves. This lovely plant was one of the victims of the Second World War and like many other plants it was then chopped up and destroyed. I was sad to see it go as it had been a great favourite of my old boss. Care, patience and attention were lavished on all these plants. For instance, azaleas would be trained in various shapes, especially pyramids and many, many hours were spent in tying the tiny shoots with cotton to make these shapes. All this care and attention repaid in full with glorious shows of flowers and coloured foliage. There were blinds fitted to the windows and roof and I became skilled in knowing when to raise or lower these or to open or shut the windows, all skills which stood me in good stead when I started to specialize in growing large plants as in the case of cattleya portia which took me forty years to grow.

There had been many changes and mild upheavals during the years. The first big upheaval was on the death of the Old Squire, William Cornwallis Cartwright, his son and daughter-in-law, Sir Fairfax and Lady Cartwright, making many, many changes. Then, the next change came with the death of Sir Fairfax and the estate passing to the hands of his son, Richard, known (with great affection) as the Young Squire although, to me as a boy, he had been Master Dick. I had had a very happy relationship with Mr Richard Cartwright during our youth. We were both interested in cactus and, indeed, he grew a fine collection. He was a very sunny and happy young man and many were the hours we spent together around the gardens. He had a love of growing things and was interested in my work. I think it is true to say he regarded me as a friend as well as an employee of his father.

When Mr Richard married there was another big change, as I have said. The Park House, which had been partially closed came to life again when Mrs Cartwright arrived. There were visitors and parties and I was responsible for the floral decorations in the house, many, many a time I went into the lovely rooms carefully placing displays of potted flowers and foliage plants. Life was good, life was happy, but then came the Hitler War and life became very, very different.

Chapter 11

Loyalist Aynho

In my day the previously republican attitudes of Aynho people (or rather, of the Lords of the Manor) had gone, practically everyone in the village was a loyal subject of the Crown and regarded the Royal Family with great affection and esteem. Without a doubt, the King was regarded as being second only to God. Indeed, like so many other other young boys and girls I made the Scout oath to 'Honour God and the King'.

Aynho men proved their loyalty when, on the outbreak of the First World War (the war to end wars!) they volunteered to fight 'For King and Country', many did not need Earl Kitchener's finger pointing at them from a poster 'Your King and Country needs You'. Some, of course, did not return and they are remembered in a memorial in the Church.

At school we sang the National Anthem for the birthday of any member of the Royal Family and the flag was flown. We remembered Empire Day and Oak Apple Day and it was instilled in us, by parents and by teachers, that we were part of the family of this country and that we must do nothing to let down our family. We were taught of the heritage that was ours, the glory of belonging to our Nation. Perhaps that is where we have gone wrong. Perhaps we do not now instil that sense of pride in our youth and more is the pity. There were no soccer hooligans in those days and vandalism was practically unheard of.

The first Royal occasion I remember is the Coronation of King George V and Queen Mary. I suppose there had been remembrance services for King Edward but I don't remember them. My recollections of the Coronation in 1911 are somewhat vague but I do remember that we had a high tea in the Borton Farm barn which had been gaily painted for the occasion. The inside was red, white and blue and even a few years ago I saw traces of this paint when I visited the old barn which still stands to this day. As we left each child was given a tin mug with the portrait of the King and Queen embossed on the side. Would that I had mine now.

King George V and Queen Mary were regarded with very great affection and respect and this affection was shared by their children. Indeed, the first member of the Royal Family I saw was their eldest son, The Prince of Wales. He rode in the point-to-point races held a few miles away and many of us went to watch those races. Of course, the Prince was the main attraction and I am sure many of the spectators were there to see him, not the races. Many women went on that day who would normally not dream of going to horse racing and many the 'flutter' that was put on the Prince and his mount. But fortunes were not made. The Prince rode well and his horse was 'there or thereabouts' but not in the first three, so like many another, I lost my wager but no one minded. The Prince was so popular I think we felt honoured that we had been able to lose our sixpences!

Of course, there were other memories of that same Prince and I will never forget that sombre evening when the streets of Aynho were almost deserted, most villagers being glued to their radio sets to hear King Edward VIII announce to his people that he was renouncing the Throne of England as he could not face the burden without the help and comfort of 'the woman I love'. Our hearts went out to our beloved King. There were many who shed a tear, heads were shaken, some (mostly the young) felt 'something could have been arranged', a few felt he had somehow let us down, but everyone was unbelieving that the unbelievable had happened. Not long before, we had mourned the passing of his father our bluff old King George V and the accession of the young King had been heralded as the dawn of a new era.

A memory of the well loved Queen Mary remains very strong. One May morning I was told that Queen Mary might be visiting Park House on her way back to London from a weekend stay in the Midlands. Of course, all the house plants and flowers had to be renewed and this I did myself but the problem was that the outside wallflowers were past their best. This, of course, couldn't be left so the outside staff were put to clearing the wallflower bed as quickly as possible and, in their place, a thousand pot-grown geraniums were planted, still in their pots! They looked very nice indeed but, as soon as Her Majesty left they were hurriedly taken out again and returned to await normal planting time some fortnight later. Many we stood in the newly dug celery trenches, one geranium between each small celery plant. We covered them with light material as frost protection and there they stayed until the beginning of June when, all danger of frost, hopefully, past, they took their places in the summer bedding display. I wonder if Queen Mary, keen gardener that she was, wondered about geraniums being planted out so early? I guess our beloved 'Queen Mum' would have raised an eyebrow!

In 1935 came a very great occasion, the Silver Jubilee of King George V. Like every other town and village, Aynho celebrated. All the houses and streets were ablaze with flags and bunting but, more especially, with flowers. There were magnificent displays. Of course, many were in the national colours, lobelia and alyssum really came into their own to provide the blue and white for the displays. It had been arranged that there would be sports for the younger elements and an open air tea in the village square. As is all too common a happening, the weather decided not to play. Oh, how it rained! But our jollity was not to be completely lost. The outdoor events had to be cancelled but a hurried re-arrangement allowed the tea to go ahead in the village hall. Some of the older inhabitants had memories of the Jubilee of the 'Widow Queen', Victoria, and many were the stories told.

All too soon came the sad news that our King was very ill again. He had survived one serious illness and had convalesced at Bognor, which proudly became Bognor Regis. Now another illness struck and this time there was no reprieve. We listened to our radio sets. We heard the sad voice of the announcer 'The King's life is drawing peacefully to its close'. Soon, the final words 'His Majesty, King George V died . . .'

Again, like every other city, town and village, Aynho mourned its King. A service of Remembrance was held in the Church and many a flag was hung at half mast. But, of course, life had to go on. 'The King is dead, Long Live the King'.

We entered the reign of King Edward VIII with such high hopes and with the trauma of the Abdication there was a great surge of sympathy for the well-respected Duke and Duchess of York and their two little daughters. We all realised the very great burden that had been thrust upon them. They were such a devoted couple, everyone had little stories of the way the Duchess had helped the Duke to overcome his intense shyness and his stammer. Many a small girl had been called Elizabeth or Margaret Rose and news of the family was always read with kindly interest and affection.

The Coronation of King George VI and Queen Elizabeth was an occasion which anyone living in Aynho and taking part in the celebrations will never forget. The whole village was decorated. Flags and bunting proliferated throughout the village; villagers vied with each other, street against street, even house against house, to give a splendid display. Of course the Squire was not to be outdone. In those days the Grammar House was the last house in the village so, from outside the Grammar House to the entrance to Park House, a distance of some 150 to 200 yards stood a line of barrels inevitably each painted red, white and blue. In each barrel was a twenty-feet high larch pole on the top of which was a large gilt crown with a laurel wreath hanging below it. The laurel wreaths were my part of the decoration and it was with great joy I made them. Bunting and flags stretched between each pole as did electric cables with red, white and blue coloured bulbs hanging from them at frequent intervals.

The barn door at the end of the square was covered with a large Union Flag which at night was illuminated. Every inhabitant of the village was entertained by the Squire and his lady to a high tea. There was much jollity and the memorable day ended with the presentation to each and every one of a suitably inscribed album containing pictures of the village decorations, a lasting and precious momento of a special day in the life of the village.

Through the years we all followed the lives of the Royal Family with great interest. We were so proud of their steadfastness during the War. We saw newsreels in the cinema of the King with his troops, or of the Queen visiting bombed out families. We were shocked when we heard that Buckingham Palace had been bombed. It was with great pride that we saw pictures of Princess Elizabeth in the uniform of the A.T.S., we read with amusement that she was heard to say 'Oh, bother', when learning the mechanics of a car. Then we were sharing the enormous relief and joy of V.E. Day to be followed in a few weeks by V.J. Day. We again cheered the newsreels showing the celebrations in front of the Palace, I remember the great smiles on all our faces at the sight of the Royal Family waving to the crowds from the balcony, there was Princess Elizabeth looking very smart in her uniform.

Soon there was the joy of the Royal engagement. Everyone felt Prince Philip, or Lieutenant Philip Mountbatten as he was then, was a very lucky young man. I think we were all happy that it was so obviously a love match. Our King and Queen had shown us that Royalty could share the joys of happy marriage and we all prayed that the young lovers would enjoy it too. By the time of the wedding of Princess Elizabeth much of the estate had been sold and somehow there was not the same guidance in the celebrations, but, like every other village, Aynho was not to be outdone in its decorations and celebrations with street parties and other events.

It was all too soon after this joyous occasion that we heard the appalling news that our King was ill, I will never forget the day which was soon to follow. A visiting grower was with me in the orchid house when the door burst open and a white-faced man said 'Ted, we've just heard, the King is dead!' We were all stunned. No more work was done that day. People stood around in shocked groups. We were numb. Only a few days before the King had waved 'Goodbye' as his elder daughter and her young husband had left for a visit to Africa, now that daughter was our Queen. We looked in our papers at pictures of the gallant little figure, dressed in black, returning to the country she now ruled and few thought of this as the dawn of a new Elizabethan era. Our sorrow for 'The Old Queen' (Queen Mary) and for Queen Elizabeth at the loss of son and husband respectively was sincere and deep. On the day of the funeral we listened in silence whilst the voice of Richard Dimbleby and other broadcasters told us of the funeral cortege, we heard the solemn broadcast and, in our thoughts, we remembered the good man who was no longer our King.

The Coronation of Her Majesty Queen Elizabeth II was again a cause for great rejoicing. The streets and houses of

Aynho were once more decorated with bunting and flags, with flowers, pictures and lights. Of course there was the usual tea for the children with commemorative mugs and other mementoes. But many of the older people had gone and there were, by this time, many newcomers in the village and I feel that the decorations and celebrations, good though they were, did not equal those of that wonderful day – the Coronation of George VI.

By this time I was no longer living in Aynho so I had little part in the village celebrations but my wife and I made very sure that our house in Banbury was beautifully decorated as we did honour to our Queen.

Chapter 12

The Second World War and after

Not long before the outbreak of the War two things had happened which had a great effect on my gardening life. In 1937 I had wondered about my own abilities, I had always worked in the one garden, had never been away to study other methods and was, perhaps, not as experienced as I should be in my role of head gardener, a post I had held for nearly ten years. I felt that I had benefitted from the teaching of Mr Brown and other colleagues, but, for quite a while I had been self-taught, it seemed that before I could really call myself a gardener I should put myself to the test. So I enrolled as a student of International Correspondence Schools of London. For the next couple of years I studied and completed the set papers. My marks were uniformly high, the lowest percentage mark received was eighty-three, most were over ninety and for Botany, Plant Form and Function I received a maximum hundred. The outbreak of War called a halt to these studies but I felt that I had improved my standards and need have no compunction in calling myself a gardener. I had completed twenty-three papers.

Like many another gardener I had been to the Chelsea Flower Show but never to the fortnightly shows of the Royal Horticultural Society. Of course I had read all about these shows for I was an avid reader of the gardening journals. I knew about the numerous committees which met to judge both the large exhibits and individual plants. Each committee being responsible for judging the exhibits of its own subject.

The second thing to have a particular effect on my gardening life was when, in 1937, I met a Banbury business man, Mr Lennard Brummit, who was an orchid grower. By this time I had grown my first orchids and was keen to improve. Mr Brummit was the man to encourage me. Not only did he grow orchids but raised them from seed. He had gained many R.H.S. awards and, indeed, later became a judge and a member of one of the R.H.S. Orchid Committees. We became friends and through him I attended my first show. I was thrilled and amazed at the variety and quality of the plants on show and never imagined that I would have the audacity to show there myself. With the encouragement of my employer and of Mr Brummit I exhibited my first show plant in January 1938, an orchid with a larger number of blooms than usual. Mr Brummit had said that he had never seen such a fine specimen of that variety and I needed little persuasion to send it by rail addressed to the Secretary of the Royal Horticultural Society with a request that it should be placed before the Orchid Committee. Mr Brummit, who was going to the show, promised to collect the plant and bring it back after the show. You can imagine the delight with which I heard that my orchid had been awarded a Certificate of Cultural Commendation, the orchid was described as 'a specially well grown specimen of *Laelia anceps*'. This award is made to the grower unlike the Award of Merit Certificate which is awarded to the plant.

During the next two years I continued to enter plants and was awarded a total of four more certificates, one silver medal and one bronze. Then, the 'phoney' war coming to an end and the real hostilities escalating, the Hall was closed for the duration, orchid growing took a back seat and the quest for food began in earnest.

A very big change came in July 1940. Mr Cartwright suggested that I should run the kitchen garden and the greenhouses on my own account as a market gardener. We agreed that this should be for the duration of the war. This was a verbal agreement, no documents were drawn up, no legal haggling just a gentleman's agreement between employer and employee. Such was the trust and faith which existed between Mr Cartwright and me, his gardener. To ensure that the continuity of my service with the Cartwright family should not be broken Mr Cartwright said that he would continue to buy my insurance stamps and to pay me a small weekly wage, for this I would care for the part of the pleasure gardens not taken over by the army. Mr Cartwright also insisted that any fruit, vegetables or flowers needed for the house would be bought from me. This arrangement was honoured by us both, until, in 1947, I handed back the gardens, greenhouses and business and once again became Head Gardener.

For the first few months of the war I was entirely without labour and was glad to rely on the help of my wife and my son, John, still a schoolboy. During those days I started work each morning at 7.0am after I had listened to the news on the radio, I kept working until just before 9pm finishing just in time to hear the final news bulletin. Of course I had to concentrate on food production. Plants which had purely decorative functions gave away to tomatoes and other such produce. Reluctantly other adjustments had to be made. All vine rods except the Muscat of Alexandria had to be cut out.

Every Sunday evening I walked through the greenhouses and around the kitchen garden making a list of the essential tasks to be done in the following week. The list was pinned up in the potting shed and, as each task was completed, it was crossed off. Sometimes the list seemed endless, especially when Home Guard duties intervened and I felt I must make up the time, working even later into the night.

During the summer evenings I was able to get a little casual help, this was used to grub out the beech and privet hedge surrounding the frame yard with two-fold benefit. The twice yearly clipping was no longer needed and more land was available for food production. A few weeks before this hedge was uprooted I had watched the remarkable process of a cuckoo being hatched. There had been a sparrow's nest containing four eggs, a few days later a fifth, much larger, egg appeared. I watched daily and eventually the young birds were hatched, first the sparrows then the cuckoo. Soon I saw that the sparrows had been forced out of the nest and were lying dead on the ground below, there was just the one bird left, a rather ugly speckled bird in sole possession of the nest which, even at that early age he nearly filled. The poor adult sparrows were frantically trying to appease the hunger of their 'baby', who always clamoured for more. The imposter continued to grow until he almost overbalanced when on the top of the nest, finally, to the undoubted relief of his foster parents he flew away.

Another sacrifice was of the peaches and nectarines which grew at the front of the lean-to greenhouses, this space was used for tomatoes which were in very great demand. Of course, our usual supplies from the Channel Islands and from Holland were not available so home grown tomatoes were welcome.

I soon learned many tricks to save time. When picking blackcurrants I pruned and gathered the fruit in one operation, by cutting the fruiting branches with the fruit attached it was possible to pick the fruit later, perhaps when too dark to see to do other jobs or when rain made outside work impossible.

Early potatoes were another paying crop. I always tried to be able to start lifting them at least a fortnight before the villagers' crops were ready, that way I was able to sell all that I could grow. I commenced planting in March covering the young shoots as soon as they showed above ground with a thin layer of straw. This was a nightly job and quite time-consuming.

It was in 1942 that I received an intriguing letter from the Peninsular Bulb Company of Sebring, Florida. I had received some Awards of Merit from the R.H.S. for hippeastrums and the letter asked me to sell them any of my best varieties but especially the two white ones, 'Snow White' and 'E. Humphris'. By this time I couldn't take up the offer, for I had but a few stock plants left, all else being scrapped to make way for the production of food. Incidently, the letter was signed, 'Yours for Victory, J. Mitchell.'

It was during these dark days that I also was grateful that I had declined another offer I had received. During the late 1930s I had been offered the job of manager at a fruit farm in Jersey. The salary offered was very, very tempting and, had I not had such a wonderful relationship with my employer or such a love for my gardens, I would have been more tempted, my wife and I often expressed our thankfulness that we resisted the temptation to move. Many years later I watched on television the series *The Enemy at the Door* and was even more thankful; now forty-odd years after the liberation I am yet more thankful!

For the first few months of the war, life had changed very little. The one excitement had been the formation of the Local Defence Volunteer Force. Then came a small detachment of officers and men from the nearby Royal Air Force Camp. The house became the home of these men, the officers having the rooms of the butler and housekeeper whilst the other ranks had the servants' quarters.

A little later into the war it was decided that Aynho should become a depot for the storage of oil and petrol for the War Office, the Air Force detachment left and the military authorities took over. The first men to arrive were from the Pioneer Corps. The outer kitchen garden, the orchard and all ground outside the inner kitchen garden walls was commandeered as was part of Aynho Park House. Officers lived in the House, the men were temporarily housed or rather tented, along the Lime Avenue until more permanent quarters were erected.

Thousands of reinforced concrete slabs started to arrive as did the materials for making Nissen huts. These huts were put in the orchard, in the Park and in the Rector's orchard. When all was ready, or nearly so, a large detachment of the Royal Army Service corps arrived. A large canteen was erected in which some fine E.N.S.A. concerts were subsequently given.

On its formation I had enlisted in the Local Defence Volunteer Force, later to be called the Home Guard. Our chief role at the outbreak of war was to act as look-outs to report the expected invasion from the air. We had no uniform and our only identification was an arm band bearing the letters L.D.V., we had no weapons either. Our special task was to watch the air over the Cherwell Valley through which ran the main London to Birmingham railway line with its long and vulnerable viaducts and the entrance to Ardley tunnel. We kept our vigil from the top of the Church tower, each day two men took up position one hour before to one hour after sunrise and in the evening one hour before to one hour after sunset. I enjoyed many beautiful sunsets from that lofty position and sunrises too, some I will never forget such were the indescribable colours which constantly changed across the sky.

It could be a boring job, and a very cold one. Even in summer the hour before dawn can be very chilly. We used to watch the village waken. I remember on several occasions as dawn approached my companion and I would have a small wager on which chimney would emit the first wisp of smoke. This usually occurred around 5.30, there were three chimneys, of which my father's was one, from which this first wisp usually appeared.

Perhaps we were not quite like *Dad's Army* but some of the stories in that series are not so far-fetched as one might imagine, just slight exaggertions perhaps! I remember one incident which happened at Aynho. One of our members suffered from poor eyesight and he mistook a flock of wild geese for a squadron or two of enemy aircraft. Yelling 'Look at the buggers coming' he made off to ring the Church bell which was the signal for invasion. Fortunately his companion had good eyesight and recognised the 'squadron' for what it was, he was able to restrain his excited colleague and so prevented the Aynho L.D.V. from becoming the laughing stock of the district.

Later I became Sergeant Major and one of my duties was to accompany the regular army instructor with a squad of new recruits on their first practice with live ammunition. One particular recruit was extremely nervous and his hands were shaking alarmingly as he tried to pull out the pin in a live grenade. The instructor whispered to me to 'Get ready quick to pick it up and get rid of it should he drop it', I must admit I did not feel very brave or happy at the prospect and was thankful when the recruit completed his task and the exercise was completed without mishap.

Eventually I was placed in charge of the Company's Spicket Mortar team. I derived great satisfaction from this new pastime but it took up a great deal of what little spare time I had. By the time war ended even a small squad like that of Aynho was well trained and could and would have given a good account of themselves had it been necessary. We proved this in one exercise. The Army stationed in Aynho were to defend the centre of the village, we were to attack but the Aynho Home Guard knew every nook and cranny and we broke the Army defence lines.

It was not until two years after the cessation of hostilities that the Army finally left Aynho Park. Although this quiet corner of Northamptonshire had been far removed from the world's battlegrounds it had not entirely escaped the ravages of war. The surrounding parkland was pock-marked with abandoned concrete emplacements, empty Nissen huts, petrol stores and dumps and we mourned the loss of many beautiful trees, spacious lawns and rose gardens which had been sacrificed to the cause of peace. We had entered into a new era and, like so many other stately homes and country estates, Aynho Park would never be the same again.

So, in March 1947, I handed the gardens back and ceased

to be a market gardener and met one of my greatest challenges, to try to put the garden back into something like its former glory. In 1940 and 1941 much of the estate had been sold. Most of the village houses had been bought by their tenants. Some houses were sold for as little as £40.00; the house in which I was born was sold for £300 to a friend of my parents who allowed them to stay on as tenants. After my father died in 1947 my mother left the house which had been her home for so long and moved to a smaller house. The owner then began to modernise it, he replaced the thatched roof with tiles and installed indoor sanitation and water. Until then most houses in the village had had outside privies and I remember an amusing story about these 'little houses at the end of the garden'.

My wife, when a girl, had gone to the privy in the dark and had been terrified to see two eyes staring up from the pit. She rushed indoors and her mother fetched a neighbour for help. It was found that a cat had fallen in. The neighbour got his scoop, a long handled shovel used to empty the privy, and scooped the cat from the odorous mess, whereupon the cat shot off at great speed. 'Someone will be a bit upset when he gets home' said the neighbour. And he was, on arriving home he found the cat on his hearthrug trying to clean himself!

But, back to my old home. The new owner did much work on it and a few years later it was sold again, this time the new owner carried out still more improvements so that when it was again sold, in 1969, it fetched in the region of £14,000. In 1975 the old house came on the market again and was sold for over £30,000.

Aynho had always been a proud and rather special village and now people with means are able to buy and afford to restore these lovely old homes, usually leaving the interesting walls, fireplaces etc, and so keep the old charm but with modern conveniences.

During the early 1950s, Aynho Park House and the pleasure grounds were opened to the public and once again I was required to provide the plants and flowers for the decoration of the house. It was desired that it should be seen not as a museum or exhibition but for what it was – a fine country residence which remained a home, a home that was lived in. Many were the floral displays which I arranged for the welcome of the visitors, many the plant I grew with good foliage and a fine head of flowers to take its place in a display for the delight of all who saw it.

Many rare and beautiful trophies were prominently displayed in the rooms of the ground floor. The dining table was laid with a glittering assembly of gold plate, silver gilt, porcelain and glass, even plates of the famous Meissen dinner service were sometimes displayed on the table. In the centre was always a tall gilt cup and cover presented by King George III to General William Cartwright on his retirement as King's Equerry, a post he had held for thirty years. The cup is inscribed 'May it a lasting monument remain of dear regard'.

During the war years my wife and I worked hard and long, we had also saved our money. It had always been our ambition that we would one day own our own house and this we achieved in January 1945. A nice house with equally nice garden became for sale in nearby Banbury, it did not have vacant possession but this did not worry us, in fact, we were quite pleased about this because it had taken all our money to buy this house and getting rent for it now would mean having something to spend when we finally did take up residence. However, in September 1945, my tenant gave me notice that she would be leaving the house, this put me in something of a quandary because empty houses were requisitioned by the local authorities. My wife and I discussed the situation and decided to ask Mr Cartwright if he would allow us to leave the bothy and to live in our own house. So, for the first time in my life, I moved into a house which I actually owned. Now I felt that, whatever else happened, I would have a home for my wife and son.

On the evening of 30 March 1954 a great tragedy was imminent, a tragedy which would affect the future of Aynho Park and the lives of all of us closely connected with the

Cartwright family. Mr Richard Cartwright and his only son, Edward, who was then aged seventeen, were both killed instantly in a motor car accident. It happened almost in sight of Aynho when they were returning from London. The news shocked the whole countryside and after the funeral the house was closed for several weeks.

The ensuing days were very sad indeed. I was kept very busy making some of the many beautiful floral tributes for the funeral. I was one of the bearers and helped to carry Mr Cartwright, my boyhood friend and manhood employer and friend, to his last resting place which was beside his father. This tragedy ended the unbroken male succession which had lasted for over three hundred years.

In November 1967 Lady Cartwright, mother of Richard and widow of Sir Fairfax Cartwright, died. By this time Mrs Cartwright and Miss Elizabeth had already left Aynho so, for the first time in three hundred and fifty years, there was no Cartwright living in Aynho.

But these sadnesses were still far away. I worked and developed my skills as a gardener and especially as a grower of pot plants and orchids but more of that in the next chapter.

Chapter 13

The 'awarding' years

My son, John, was born on 30 October 1928 and was a source of great pride and joy to me. At five years old he went to the village school, the one I had joined when only three some twenty-eight years before. He gained a scholarship to Banbury Grammar School where he joined the A.T.C. Just before he was sixteen he gained a place in the Royal Air Force to train as a pilot but was unable to continue – poor John, his dreams of being a pilot floundered when he suffered continual air-sickness. A pilot's life was not for him.

He was then conscripted for two years which he served in the Horse Guards (I should tell you, John is a very tall man!) He served in Germany and it was during a leave from Germany that he married Sheila. John and Sheila gave me a grandson, Paul, who has in turn married and given me two great grandchildren, Roisin and Russell. After his compulsory two years John left the Army with the rank of King's Corporal and then joined the Metropolitan Police with whom he served for twenty-five years before retiring with the rank of Inspector.

He still lives in Banbury, a couple of miles from my own home as do my grandson and his family.

From the earliest days in my gardening career I was irresistibly attracted to the hybridization of plants. It is such a pity that more people do not try this fascinating aspect of horticulture but remain satisfied to produce plants grown from someone else's seeds.

My first attempt to procure my own seed was in crossing hippeastrums, so often called amaryllis. Because the flowers are so large these are amongst the easiest to cross. When the seeds were ripe I sowed twelve seeds in a four inch pot in a compost of leaf-soil, peat and silver sand. I have always preferred to grow seed in pots rather than pans or boxes, it is so much easier to turn a rooted seedling from a pot without damage to the roots.

I potted on the seedlings in small pots in a compost of good, fibrous loam, peat, decayed cow-manure, silver sand and a little crushed charcoal, the whole rubbed through a half-inch sieve. It is the natural wish of any grower to flower his seedlings as soon as possible so he must keep them growing without a check of any sort and never allow them to become root bound. I always repotted as soon as the roots reached the sides of the pot, giving them as small a shift as possible. Sometimes I did a top dressing too. As the seedlings became larger I included more loam in their soil, their final compost consisting of three parts good, fibrous loam, one part peat and one part decayed cow manure. To each barrow load of this mixture I would add one ten-inch pot of mortar rubble and a similar amount each of coarse silver sand and crushed charcoal together with one six-inch pot of bone meal. A varied and healthy diet!

Once established the bulbs were repotted every five years, in the years between they were top dressed with a compost containing a good fertilizer. It is the little details that make all the difference between success and failure, perhaps the two most important points in the successful cultivation of hippeastrums, or indeed of any plant, are very careful watering and keeping the plants clean. Cleanliness cannot be stressed too strongly, many batches of plants are ruined by mealy bug and thrips which result from lack of cleanliness. If a plant is not clean it is not healthy.

As I have already said, one can easily produce hippeastrum seed, the size of the flowers makes it very simple to remove the anthers when the flowers are half open, then, when fully open the stigma is ready for fertilization with ripe pollen from another flower.

Thousands, perhaps millions of hippeastrums are sold every year in their dormant stage. The majority will produce a flower spike or perhaps two in the first year, it is after the first year that many people find difficulty in producing flowers. Like all bulbs, the hippeastrum must first flower and then have a resting period. As soon as the flower spike is visible, usually in late winter or very early spring, the plant should be well watered and this should be continued until the flowers fade. When the flower is dead it should be cut off close to the top of the stem and watering continued alternating between liquid manure and clear water until the leaves turn yellow. Water should gradually be reduced until the leaves die right down. The compost should then be kept dry until the next year when a flower spike will again be visible. The whole of the flower stem should remain after the flower has been broken off, the goodness in the stem and leaves will return to the bulb as they die down. Finally, when quite dead the stem and leaves will come away with a gentle pull. Sunshine is also necessary at this time. If no sunny window is available, and not everyone wants dying plants on their window sill, the bulb can be put outside in August and September but only if a sunny, sheltered position is available. Ideally the pots should be put into a large hole in the ground which has been half filled with coarse gravel, this will allow good drainage and prevent the plant becoming waterlogged. Put a small piece of slate on the gravel with a few matchsticks on it, this will prevent worms from entering the compost and allow drainage.

This attention which I bestowed on my hippeastrums was

fully rewarded when I exhibited my best plants at the Royal Horticultural Hall – I gained three Awards of Merit Certificates and the Silver Banksian Medal.

It was during the first few years after I became head gardener and sold the surplus produce that I supplied fruit for royalty, one king and a future king. The first Earl of Birkenhead lived nearby at The Cottage, Charlton, and I was asked to supply grapes, peaches, nectarines, figs, pears etc. My mother-in-law was cook-housekeeper and knew that any fruit I provided would be of the best. The guests were the then Duke of York who brought a tennis party from Oxford to play a team of Lord Birkenhead and his friends. Of course, the Duke of York became King George VI, the other 'royal' who ate my fruit was ex-King George of Greece.

These occasions were exciting for all concerned. My father-in-law was butler to Mrs Myres at The Lodge at Charlton and he was called in to help his friend, Mr Trowbridge at The Cottage. Even my wife was roped in to help in the pantry and was given a decanter which had been used at the party, this I still have. I was allowed to be an interested spectator to the dinner preparations. The fish course was a whole salmon beautifully cooked and decorated, the main course was a ham, partly cooked then skinned and covered with brown sugar, then continuously basted with champagne. The main sweet was a special souffle which looked beautiful. Just before being taken to the dining room it was covered with a golden mist made from boiling brown sugar which was thrown into the air to settle as a mist on the souffle. With some of the maids I stood on one of the top landings to listen to the after dinner speeches. On other occasions we had visits from many famous people and my wife and I heard Sir Winston Churchill and Sir John Simon amongst others.

There was one tragedy with a visitor to Aynho, she was a deaf lady who, having been taken to the station, crossed the track in front of a train. It wasn't the slow, stopping train which she had been intending to catch but an express. My wife, son and I were witnesses to this dreadful accident. I ran shouting to warn her but her deafness prevented her hearing my shouts and she was flung to the platform and killed instantly.

But to return to the fruit I supplied to these parties, it had to be very carefully chosen and pears were the most difficult to choose. It is extremely difficult to know exactly when a pear is at its best, one can look perfect on the outside but inside it can have become 'sleepy', or the skin and flesh may feel just right and the centre still be rock hard. Mr Cartwright always said 'You're sure these pears are all right, aren't you? I don't want my guests finding them less than perfect.' I chose peaches by first examining them carefully, then with the palm of one hand under the fruit I would make a slight impression with the tip of a finger of the other hand at the point when the fruit joined the branch. If I judged it ready I would pick by an upward movement and sharp twist to the fruit.

Pears require a certain amount of experience to know when they are at their very best. I judged them right when the nail of my finger would just penetrate the skin around the nose of the fruit, I could almost guarantee that the fruit would be sweet and melting, right to the core.

One of the most exciting days of my life was a day in February 1938 when I experienced the enormous thrill and satisfaction of seeing a plant I had grown amongst those on the rostrum of awards at the Royal Horticultural Society fortnightly show. On this occasion the plant was the hippeastrum I had named after young Mr Edward Cartwright. Of course, I had previously won an award with an orchid but on that occasion I had sent the plant by train and was not present to see it on show.

On the last occasion in 1940 that the show was held I took three plants of the regal pelargonium, Carmine. I had hoped to gain a Certificate of Cultural Commendation but to my great surprise and joy the plants not only gained that award but also an Award of Merit Certificate. I had started these pelargoniums from a cutting brought to me by my doctor who knew I was interested in hybridization. His remark on giving me the cutting was 'See what you can do with this', the result, after a goodly number of years, was this beautiful pelargonium which gained me these two R.H.S. Awards.

I suppose I am not the only grower who has made one cardinal mistake. Thinking I was just following a hobby and not thinking I might raise something very special, I did not keep records of the crosses I made in my plants. This was a terrible blunder; I have grown a zonal pelargonium, a regal pelargonium and three hippeastrums which have all received awards of merit but, because of my lapse, I cannot state the exact parentage. As I have said – a terrible blunder.

This particularly applies to the pelargonium Elizabeth Cartwright which gained an Award of Merit in 1950 receiving all twenty votes, this, a truly beautiful deep red created a great deal of interest. It was with this pelargonium that, in December of the same year, I was awarded the Sanders Gold Medal for the best new greenhouse plant of general utility. I just cannot describe the joy and excitement I felt when I heard of this award, especially as it is usually awarded for a rather exotic plant.

It was a year or so after I won this award that I was visited by the managing director of the Ryder Seed Company. I gave him a conducted tour of the greenhouses and pleasure grounds and told him the history of the house. I talked of the people I worked for, the people I worked with, of the village and my place in it. Thanking me for such a pleasant and interesting afternoon he told me that he had really come to see me to persuade me to leave Aynho and to go to their nursery to raise nothing but pelargoniums. Indeed, I suppose one can say he wanted to turn me into the Russell of pelargoniums, there might have been Humphris pelargoniums as there are Russell lupins. However, he realised that my heart was truly in my plants, the village and in Aynho Park House so he guessed my answer would be 'No'. Not even the promise that the seeds would be marketed as the Aynho House Strain with my photograph on every packet would persuade me to move.

Realising that I had something special I began to increase my stock of the Elizabeth Cartwright plant, I told Mr Cartwright that it seemed a pity to confine such a lovely pelargonium to Aynho. Mr Cartwright replied quite simply, 'They are your creations, you must exploit them.' This brought up the subject of money as, technically, the plants belonged to my employer. Again, Mr Cartwright behaved magnificently, 'Any money you get is yours'.

So, in my spare time I began to increase my plants and, in 1952, a well-known authority and specialist on pelargoniums came to see me wanting to buy the whole of my stocks but this I refused to allow. However, I said that if we could agree on a price I would sell some and not part with any of mine for a period of three years. I had nearly one hundred plants of the Elizabeth Cartwright to part with and thought £100 a fair price. This man wanted to pay not more than £50.00 and I offered him fifty for that leaving me to sell the others where I wished. This was not to his liking, he did not want a competitor. Finally we came to an agreement, I would let him have the lot for £50.00 and take twenty-five percent on all sales for the first three years. It would have paid him to have given me the £100 I asked for as he sold almost one hundred in the first year at £1.00 each. I was told that the plants were sold in thirteen countries. Subsequently I sold the same man some of my other award winning varieties.

Having a large house to decorate with plants and flowers was a challenge. The right plants had to be selected and grown on, they had to be free flowering and of good shape and fine, specimen quality plants are not the result of just one or two years work but the result of several years. To illustrate my point I had a small plant of the orchid Brassocattleya 'Viscountess Weir' with one bloom in 1938, twenty years later it carried ten blooms when it gained a Certificate of Cultural Commendation and in 1968 the same plants carried thirty-six perfect blooms and gained a second certificate.

But the most exciting of all my plants must be my Cattleya Portia. I first showed this plant before the war when, on my first showing at the R.H.S. I gained an award. Portia was also responsible for one of my disappointments, although the sadness was not of long duration. I had shown three plants of Portia between them carrying one hundred and ninety lovely blooms. They came down from the committee rooms and I was a little disappointed to see that they had received a Certificate of Cultural Commendation. You may think this should have pleased me, well it did, but I had secretly cherished the hope that they might gain a Bronze Lindley Medal. These medals of which there are bronze, silver and silver gilt are very special medals which, so I understood, could be awarded only by the full Council of the Royal Horticultural Society. I was aiming high! The medals can be awarded either for exquisite beauty or for exceptional skill in cultivation. I suppose my disappointment must have shown in my face because one of the stewards came across to me and told me that the Certificate award was only temporary, a far greater award had been recommended, I waited with bated breath as one of the stewards took the card away from my plants and replaced it, to my enormous joy, with a card saying that the Lindley Medal had been awarded.

The show now had little interest for me, all I wanted to do

was to sit near my plants and listen to the comments and remarks of the people. Not even ten years later when I again showed three plants, this time carrying over five hundred blooms and for which I was awarded the Silver Lindley Medal, did I experience the incredible thrill, joy and satisfaction that I had felt on that earlier afternoon. One of my friends jokingly said 'You'll have to buy a bigger hat', I hope I was not too big-headed but I do remember telling him that I was amazed at my own courage the first time I exhibited at these prestigious shows. Having seen the wonderful variety of plants at these shows and seen the skilful way in which they were presented I think perhaps it was a good thing that I sent my first exhibit by rail before I had ever attended a show. I am sure I would not have dared to exhibit had I visited the shows beforehand. I think, too, that had my first plant not received an award I would have felt like hiding away because of my presumption. I have told a great deal more about Cattleya Portia in my other book, *Garden Glory*, so will not dwell on it here.

Of course, I had some near disasters. One was in 1941 when a burst pipe meant that I was without heat for two days and nights. There was the blackout to worry about so I borrowed a large rick sheet to cover the roof then, with one electric heater and two paraffin stoves I managed to save my plants but not the blooms. It was at least two years before the plants finally recovered.

Looking back at my gardening career I don't think I had a complete failure, at least, not one that was the result of something I failed to do or did wrongly. But I had my share of disappointment. One disappointment I will always remember. In the late 1930s I had developed a hippeastrum to which I had given my wife's name, Zarita. This plant was the result of a cross between two Award of Merit varieties, one was a large rose pink with which I had gained an Award in February 1938, the other variety was 'Susan' which I had been told had won an award in 1936. Zarita was a beautiful plant which resembled Susan more than my variety. To get an award it had, in the opinion of the judges, to be a distinct advance on Susan. The judges did not think it was and so Zarita did not get an award. I still think that my plant was an advance, the blooms were quite a lot larger and the colour equally as good. I have often shown slides of the two blooms and have invited people to choose the better. Always Zarita has been chosen.

Having won the Silver Lindley Medal for my orchid (which by now were being known as 'The Aynho Orchids') I received many letters and visits from people interested in them. In January 1960 my plants were shown on television, but in black and white. This gave me three ambitions. The first was to build a box around the three plants to encourage them to grow together as one plant. The second wish was to have the plants again on television, but this time in colour, the third ambition was to have a thousand blooms. The first two ambitions were realised but the third, which I had estimated would take a further four or five years, was completely dashed when most of the leaves were scorched by the sun. In those days, which was some time after the death of Mr Cartwright, I was travelling to Amersham to the new home of Mrs Cartwright, who was now Mrs Hoare. For a few weeks I had help only from a retired railway man who came in every afternoon from 2.0 until 5.0, on the days I went to Amersham he came in at 10.0 until 12.0 as well. Usually, before making the forty mile trip to Amersham I would lower the blind, but that morning, when I left at 7.30 it was raining and thinking that my colleague would lower the blind I left it. Unfortunately, he didn't until after the damage had been done. It was a bitter disappointment as I did not have time to recoup the loss.

In the dark days of winter I seldom saw my home in daylight except on Sundays and Saturday and Thursday afternoons when I left at 4.0. It was on one such Thursday that I was standing at the bus stop in Aynho when a car drew up. Two Aynho ladies got from the car saying 'Ted, this gentleman is going through Banbury and will give you a lift.' I was extremely grateful and climbed into the car, I thanked the driver who then admired a bunch of chrysanthemums which I

147

was carrying. I immediately recognised his voice and said 'Good Lord, Percy Thrower'. Inevitably we started talking flowers. Percy was eager to hear about Portia and before I had time to tell him everything we were at Banbury. He was most disappointed that he could not stop for a longer talk but, as I got out of the car he said 'We shall certainly meet again', and we did, in the Birmingham Television Studio!

Chapter 14

Some small measure of fame

My plant's first appearance on television came in 1960 when
my orchid was shown, this plant had by now become quite
famous but it is interesting to recall how it came into my care.
The original was bought in the early 1920s at Harrods by
Lady Cartwright. It is quite certain that she had no idea (and
neither did I!) that this plant would be shown on television –
what was television in 1920? Lady Cartwright was always
interested in the plants and was impressed with the way this
one grew, I was so very pleased that she lived to see much of
the fame which her purchase achieved. From a small plant
carrying about eight blooms in 1920 to one with one hundred
and ninety in 1938 and five hundred and twenty-six blooms in
1948. When it was shown on television it carried over eight
hundred blooms.

In January 1960 came my first TV appearance and then in
August 1960 came my second which was part of a broadcast
from the Radio and Television Show at Earls Court presented
by Cliff Lewis. I took a number of plants from Aynho and had
a fascinating and tiring day answering many questions and
talking with many gardeners. I was glad son John had come

along too, he was still in the Metropolitan Police Force and had the policeman's presence. He answered many questions and eased our day quite considerably.

The next time I was on television was in Gardening Club January 1961, Paul Morby was the producer and I had a truly interesting time being given the chance to follow all stages of the presentation. I realised just how much work goes into the presentation for so short a programme. My next appearance was tele-recorded on a Friday for showing on Sunday afternoon in the usual Gardening Club programme. This was a particularly interesting programme, Percy Thrower introduced it and spent the first ten minutes talking about vegetable growing problems before joining me in the greenhouse. One of the interesting aspects of this programme was that there was an audience with whom my wife and I shared a cocktail party after the show.

More television and radio programmes followed and I began to get letters from many interested and interesting people. These letters came from as far afield as America, Malaysia and Australia. Of course, I continued propagating, hybridizing and generally growing plants which could be used as decoration. I continued to show at the Royal Horticultural Society Shows and won a total of twenty-five awards in thirty shows over a period of twenty-five years.

Gradually the idea began to form that perhaps I should write a book. Many books have been written about gardens and gardeners but few by a gardener himself. This is not suprising for in those days few gardeners had much time for the pen and paper preferring the spade and fork. So, during my precious spare time and with the help and encouragement of my wife and John I started to jot down ideas and items for a book. I think anyone who had been born at the turn of the century could find material for a book. I lived in stirring times. I lived during the early days of the motor car, when the first aeroplane flew, I saw the early radios and then television, there were changes in medicine, in education – even in gardening! Of course there was space flight and men on the moon. There were ugly things too, wars and disasters – but we won't dwell on those.

It was whilst my ideas were turning to writing that I celebrated fifty years at Aynho Park. Thanks to the wonderful generosity of Mr Richard Cartwright in continuing to buy my insurance stamps and to pay me a small wage during my years as market gardener I had qualified for a long service award of The Royal Horticultural Society with which I was presented on 7 April 1959 to celebrate forty-three years. At that time two hundred and one awards were made with sixteen to gardeners with fifty years service and thirteen with sixty years! I felt a positive beginner with my forty-three years! Most of the medals were presented at a ceremony at Vincent Square, Westminster by the President of the R.H.S., The Hon. David Bowes-Lyon.

But to return to my book. I wrote it and then came up against the hazard known to all would-be authors. It is comparatively easy to write the book, the problems come with trying to find a publisher. I first sent my manuscript to Faber & Faber (I had been told that they had a very good book-list on gardening topics). Fabers showed some interest and asked me to go to London to discuss the matter with them. This I did, they made various suggestions, which I followed but then, after I had done the work as suggested they sent the manuscript back saying that it did not fit in with their list of gardening books.

I think I would have let the matter rest there but fate was to intervene. On the very sad day on which Lady Cartwright was buried I was introduced to a Scottish lady who, having heard that I had written a book expressed a wish to read it. Although my manuscript was not properly typed, being partly hand-written, nevertheless she liked it and passed it on to a friend of hers who happened to be Sir William Collins of the famous publishing house. I was delighted to get a letter from Sir William saying that his firm would be happy to publish *Garden Glory*. They were so sure that the book would sell they paid me a sum on the signing of the contract and a further sum on publication. The print run was seven and a half thousand copies and over two thousand were sold in the first three weeks with a further hundred sold abroad. The entire run was sold in less than two years. I am now told that second-hand copies are much in demand. Indeed, our local Banbury Bookshop continually advertises for the book and recently sold three which they had obtained. My book was advertised in the gardening magazines and was featured in an article in the *Sunday Times*. After the publication I appeared on both the B.B.C. and the A.T.V. in news or current affairs programmes.

My book led me to be asked to speak at gardening clubs, orchid clubs, political clubs, clubs for the over-sixties, churches, chapels and just about every other club where members might be interested in gardening. Indeed, although I am now well into my eighties I still give talks. I have a fine collection of slides which I show. Sometimes I talk only of the orchids, sometimes of other plants, sometimes of my gardening life in general. I hope I may be able to continue these talks for some time yet – my healthy out-door life has kept me quite fit even if arthritis is beginning to make its nasty presence felt.

For twenty-one years after I moved to Banbury I travelled to and from Aynho, a distance of six miles each way. During all my years at Aynho I seldom had a day off work apart from my half day a week and every Sunday, at least, every Sunday in later years when the 'duty' system meant that I paid my assistant to do the Sundays for me. I had never missed a day because of illness until January 1963 when I became ill and was away a whole month. It was a truly worrying time for me as the weather was extremely severe but, perhaps to alleviate my worries it was then I started to think about writing the book – so even from bad things good can come. My convalescence was helped by reading old diaries, newspaper cuttings and letters.

But the time was fast approaching when the last ties between Aynho gardens and Ted Humphris would be severed. At least, the physical ties, nothing will ever sever the ties in my heart. Miss Elizabeth Cartwright and her mother decided to sell the greenhouses and gardens which were bought by a local businessman and I sadly handed over the keys for the last time. But my work was not quite finished. Miss Cartwright had bought a beautiful old house in the West Country and some of the garden treasures were to be moved.

So, in the Spring of 1969 I began the task of dismantling the famous orchid Cattleya Portia for transport to its new home. You can imagine the poignant thoughts which persisted. The plant had been contained in a box fifteen feet by five feet but had to be divided into smaller containers for its transfer to the West Country. We hired a two-tier cattle truck which was filled with the cattleya and other plants. I find it difficult to describe my feelings as I walked through the now empty greenhouses. Floods of memories came to me, I remembered the awe and wonder of a small boy on seeing strawberries ripening in pots high on the shelves whilst snow was on the ground outside. I remembered the dear colleagues (and one or two not so dear) with whom I had worked. I remembered the Old Squire, Sir Fairfax Cartwright and Lady Cartwright, whose love of flowers and plants had given me such impetus and encouragement. I remembered 'Young Mr Richard', I was reminded of the time when one of the other boys said 'Come and see what Mr Richard has got', and there, in an enclosure was a kangaroo! I remembered Mr Richard Cartwright, squire, employer, friend and encourager, I remembered his wife, Elspeth, who also gave me such friendship, and who, after a period of widowhood had married Mr Eustace Hoare, and so I remembered Mr Hoare, another fine gentleman and splendid employer whose sad death had been such a loss. And I remembered Miss Elizabeth, I had known her as a baby, a toddler, a school-girl and a lovely young lady and I hoped she would be happy in her new home. I felt sad that the Cartwrights were part of Aynho no more.

I looked at the bothy. The home I shared with colleagues and then with my dear wife, I hoped the new owner would be as happy there as I had been. But life had to go on.

One period of sadness could not take from me the enormous joy and pleasure my work had given me, so, in handing over the keys, I felt both sadness and satisfaction, sadness that the work was done but satisfaction in the knowledge that I had done my best. Satisfaction was mine in a happy and rewarding career.

Chapter 15

After 'Garden Glory'

One of the greatest rewards in writing a successful book was the number of pen friends I made, not only in this country but from other parts of the world. I received very, very many letters. One was from a Mrs Jan Cherneaviky of Vancouver, British Columbia who wrote that after reading *Garden Glory* she felt she must travel again to England (in spite of the multitudes of people) just to see Aynho. Another letter came from Mrs Scott Alden of Tennessee, U.S.A., her letter came during Jubilee Year and ended 'God Bless your lovely Queen, a credit, not only to England but to the whole civilised world'.

A letter which gave me particular pleasure was from Mr Robert A. Humphris of Victoria, Australia. He wrote that the daughter of a cousin had been in England and had seen my book on sale so had bought it having been attracted by the identical spelling of our surname. He and some of his relatives were engaged in trying to trace their ancestors and felt there was a possibility that we might be related. The name is usually spelt with an 'E' – Humphries – so it is possible that anyone spelt as my name is, may be descended from just one family. It is an interesting thought. Who knows, perhaps way back in history a member of the Humphries or Humphreys

155

may have fallen out with his clan and so dropped the 'E', an intriguing thought!

Robert Humphris has traced back to a Richard Francis Humphris who married a widow named Spiers of Southleigh, Oxfordshire, in 1752. He had two grandsons who emigrated to Australia in 1850 and my correspondent was descended from one of them. Mr Robert Humphris and his wife Betty paid a visit to England and spent a day with me.

It was in 1977 that I received a particularly interesting letter which came from Mrs Helen Borton Ott. This American lady told me that she had been Miss Borton and that her family had originated in Aynho. I traced that she was of the same family as old Fred Borton, the village carrier of my childhood. John Borton son of William and Elizabeth Borton had been baptised in St Michaels Church, Aynho, on 25 January, 1634. John married a girl from the neighbouring village of Croton (now Croughton) and had become a Quaker. John and his wife were the only known Borton Quakers and attended the Quaker Meeting House in the nearby village of Adderbury. You will remember, St Michaels was, and still is, the only place of worship in Aynho.

John Borton was sent to prison for his Quaker beliefs, the Quakers being sadly persecuted by the Church of England. His imprisonment began in 1660, I do not know how long this lasted but in 1679 he was forced to leave this country to start a new life in New Jersey, U.S.A. where he died in 1687, his wife, Anne, died a year later.

Mrs Borton Ott sent me many copies of papers dealing with the family, one, of very great interest, quoted the fact that the Borton family has a great claim to fame being listed in the Guinness Book of Records as having the largest family tree. This tree is painted on a canvas measuring fifteen feet by eighteen feet and weighs ten pounds. It lists the family since 1562 and contains no less than 6,820 names. At least, that was the score when that particular article was written, but that was in the *Quaker Weekly Journal* of 14 January 1977. No doubt there are more names now. Of course, this does not mean that this is the largest family in the world, or even that it can trace back further than anyone else, merely that it was the largest listing at that time.

A book sent to me by Mrs. Ott contains a chapter on 150 years of Bortons in Canada. This tells of William Borton and his wife Sarah Baldwin, both of Aynho whose sons Henry and Edmund emigrated from Aynho to settle in Canada under a scheme which was supported by the Cartwrights and which ran from 1829 to 1847.

Of course, many of the Cartwright family had also emigrated to Canada and there is a story of an encounter which I think is interesting. E.R. Cartwright C.B.E. in his book *A Late Summer* states that he arrived at the Eighth Corps Headquarters at Chateau La Lovie (during the First World War) and was taken to meet the General. His guide introduced him to the General saying 'General Cartwright, I have brought our new officer, Captain Cartwright, to meet you'. The young officer apparently made his very best salute but the General rose with outstretched hand and with a smile said 'My noble namesake'. This was the name by which the General called Mr Cartwright during the whole time they worked together. General Cartwright was one of the Canadian branch of the family.

There were other letters, some just complimentary, some asking for advice, some telling of ties with Aynho or other local villages. All these letters gave me enormous pleasure and those from Mrs Ott with their wide-ranging subjects were of particular interest, especially as I know members of her family.

There were other red letter days which followed my little piece of fame. One was the invitation to give a talk in connection with my book at Harrods. It was so very appropriate that this should have been the store from which my earliest orchid had come. There was a Harrod's Festival of Flowers held in conjunction with the Festival of London Stores and it was wonderful to be asked to speak and participate.

One of my most welcome visitors was the late Mr Godfrey Winn who spent a whole day with me, he was most interested as we journeyed around Aynho to see the different links with the past. We looked at the old causeways, the stocks and the apricot trees. He asked a great number of questions, and indeed, so did I! After his visit Mr Winn wrote an article of some three thousand words for the magazine *Woman and Home* which, so I'm told had a circulation of about three million copies around the world. The article was entitled *Fresh Fields* and contained pictures in both colour and black and white.

This was not a time of unalloyed happiness. Indeed, a very great sadness was to come to me. My dear wife, Zarita, and I had moved to a new home in Twyford, near Banbury. It is a nice house on the edge of Cherwell Valley and from the windows I can see across to Kings Sutton, the village of my own ancestors, and to Aynho, the village of my birth. It was Christmas 1971 and Zarita and I had been to several parties and dances. Christmas Day was very happy for us, we had all the family with us. On the mantlepiece stood two tickets for a New Year Dinner and Dance but we did not use them. On the morning of 29 December my wife suddenly complained of pains in her chest. The pains increased as the day wore on and late that night she was admitted to hospital. Of course I went with her to see her settled. Before I left to come home I kissed her and promised to come the next day. She said 'Ted, take care of yourself and of Mitzy'. Mitzy was a little white poodle which I had given her some time before. Those were the last words she said to me – she passed away the next morning. It was a terrible shock when the news was broken to me. I took a long, long time to come to terms with my loss but I was helped by that little dog. It was so strange but as the cortege drew up outside the house on the day of the funeral, Mitzy stood with her paws on the window sill and she stayed there for most of the next three days. It seemed she then decided her mistress would not come back for she suddenly transferred her affections to me. Many is the hour I spent with that little dog on my lap. There is a strange footnote to this. The first time I took the dog to the cemetery she went in front of me and stopped by the grave of her mistress, somehow she knew.

So, to help in my loneliness I started to jot down items of interest. I spent hours looking at my diaries, press cuttings, photographs and books. It was rather a hodge podge until my neighbour and friend offered to help me to sort them into this, my second book. To her I owe more than I can ever repay.

There are so many aspects of village life, so many stories to be told, so many people to remember that it has been difficult to put them into some sort of sequence. Difficult to know what is of general interest and what to leave out. Now that I am alone I do not now feel sad or unhappy. I am thankful that I have lived through a period of awe-inspiring developments, that I shared my home with a loyal and loving wife, that I made many friends, that I always did what I thought right and was in debt, for money, to no man. My debts of another kind are great. To my parents, especially to my mother for instilling in me the ethics of my life, to Mr Brown and my other colleagues for the help and encouragement they gave to a raw young gardener. To my employers for their forbearance, generosity and understanding, to the many friends and neighbours for their pleasure at my successes and to the village of my birth for its warmth and tolerance.

Writing this I am approaching my eighty-fourth birthday. I look from my window and see Aynho bathed in the evening sunlight, the village has a right to be proud of its history. Down through the ages there have been many famous sons and daughters of Aynho, this pride seems to permeate the village and I too am proud to have been born and bred in the village and to have spent my working days there.

If I have brought a small measure of fame to the village I am proud and delighted, in spite of temptations to move away, I always worked there. Now, although I live three miles away, in my heart I still feel myself to be a son of the 'Apricot Village'.

A walk round the village

It was on a hot and sultry day in the warm summer of 1984 that I drove Ted Humphris up the road to Aynho. We passed the turn to Kings Sutton and he reminded me of the times his grandfather and then his father, had walked the three miles each way to work at Aynho. Of course, in those far off days there had not been tarmac roads and indeed, they had probably taken a short cut through the fields, but it was a long walk.

As we approached the village Ted pointed to a house taller than its neighbours, 'My old home,' he said. He then asked me to slow down and, pointing to a field on the right said that there was the site of the old fish ponds. Next was College Farm. We stopped the car and looked at it. 'Once upon a time,' said Ted, 'that was a hostel or hospital for a religious order, it's been a farm for a long time though.'

We turned left into Brackley Road but not before he had pointed to the stocks further up the hill. They had been moved from their old place in the village and are now protected from vandals by a fence. Next point of interest was a wall on the left

161

behind which was the engine pond. Ted explained that this pond was unlike the usual English village pond because it was enclosed on all sides by a high wall and it had a stone paved floor. Several streams flowed into this pond, the water then flowing under the road and through a series of low arches to the engine house from whence it was pumped into large tanks on top of Aynho Park House. When the demand for water increased or when the engine was not working the task was taken over by a water ram, a type of hydraulic engine. Of course, ultimately the task was taken over by electricity until finally water mains were installed.

I heard how the pond was cleaned out every fortnight and Ted recalled standing on the steps just inside the door to watch his father and uncle scrub the stone floor with bass brooms. One of the six oil lamps which illuminated the village also stood on this corner.

Round the corner we drove to a row of houses at the end of which is the Old Malt House. Ted was dubious about when this was used for a malt house, he said 'It's too far from the Cartwright Arms for it to have been used by them, perhaps it was for the hostel,' he told me that even when he was young the landlord of the Cartwright Arms brewed his own beer as did many of the villagers. In any case, during his youth the building had been known as the Parish Barn because the parishioners stored their grain and produce grown on their allotments there.

We moved on round the corner. 'There,' said Ted 'is our recreation ground, Big Butts.' I saw a row of council houses but then I heard how this was the play area for the entire village. As its name implies, it had been the site of the archery tournaments, no doubt way back in medieval times jousting had taken place there as well. A magnificent row of elm trees had stood along the side of Big Butts, being felled in the 1950s when the land was taken for a housing estate. Ted told me that these trees had been a landmark for miles around and one which everyone in the village had loved. Philosophically Ted said that if they had not been felled in 1950 they still might have gone with 'This nasty Dutch elm disease'. We then looked at the Alms Houses which stand along the edge of what had been Little Butts, a smaller playing field and was now part of the same housing estate. We moved on to the back entrance of the Cartwright Arms and I heard stories of past landlords and how the inn was quite a centre of village life. During his childhood the yard had had a large wire cage attached to the stables in which were peacocks 'Noisy wretches' said Ted, 'but beautiful'.

We turned back and parked the car outside the tallest house in the village 'My old home' said Ted with undoubted affection. He had 'phoned in advance and the present owners, Major and Mrs Graham welcomed us to look around the ground floor of the house. It is now a very elegant and lovely home, much altered since the turn of the century, but, with Ted's graphic description I could see the house as it was. The large and beautifully furnished room used to be two small rooms, I could imagine the boys of the Humphris family in those rooms, the chimney was wide (it had been altered to avoid the dreadful draughts) but one could still imagine the children looking up the chimney to the starlit sky above. It was then that Ted made another remark that intrigued me, 'Of course, in those days there were so many more stars in the sky, you could look up and the sky would be full. But then, there wasn't all this pollution and all these satellites and things spoiling it up there.' It made me remember the starlit skies of my own childhood, not quite so long ago as Ted's but still a long while back, and I too, realised that it is a long, long time since I saw a night sky so full of stars as in my childhood. Ted was disappointed that the old 'back door' had gone, he said it had been a very heavy studded door of oak 'such as you would find in a church', now the place where that had been led to a modern kitchen which had been built on in place of an old outhouse. We went outside, Ted telling me that, although some people believed that the house had once been a threshing house, he did not believe that. He believed that the house had been part of the hostel or hospital in what is now

College Farm, he pointed out the barred windows in the upper floors and the surprising flight of steps which led from the garden to a window. It didn't need much imagination to conjure up pictures of sick people being carried down these steps, perhaps even lepers who would be fed through a hole in the wall.

We walked down the garden, past the old pig styes and I was shown the site of the 'privy'. We came to the end of the garden and Ted showed me the break in a row of cottages which backed 'his' garden. This he was sure had been an entrance to the house, it seemed logical, after all, the gap was to a main road, or one that had been 'main' in those far off days when the religious order was in residence. Mr Humphris senior had allowed the cottagers fronting the Brackley road to enclose part of his garden for their own so the theory of the entrance became even more probable.

As I have said, it was a large house, from its topmost window there was a splendid view across the Cherwell Valley. It was said that this window was used as a look-out during the Civil War but there seems some controversy as to who was watching for who! Aynho was a Parliamentarian stronghold which was captured by the royalists who held it until after the battle of Naseby, but this resident of Ted's house was alleged to be a Royalist. Did the window watcher look for the approaching Royalists to welcome them? Did he, after Naseby look for the Parliamentarians in fear? That is something we cannot know.

Ted's house stands on Blacksmith's Hill, a steep narrow road in the centre of the village. Right opposite the old home stood the blacksmith's shop where the young Ted used to help the smiths. Even as a tiny child he had sat on a stool or on a grassy bank beside his home to watch the shoeing of horses and, as he got older, to hold the horses' heads. The grassy bank is gone, there is a garage there now and the old forge is also a garage. Next to the old home there is a yard before another large cottage. This was known as Hell's Yard. 'There were,' said Ted 'two versions of the reasons for this name. One was that someone called Hell or Ell had lived there (and there are still Ells in the village), the other, much more fanciful, but possibly right, was that this would have been the area to take the first onslaught when the Royalists attacked the village.' Ted inclined to the first theory. He pointed out that there were other areas known after their one time residents. Colley's Yard for example, that had been the yard leading to Mr Colley's house, the village hall stands there now. Then there is Bennett's Corner, that was the home of the Aynho Park House butler (the only Roman Catholic in the village).

Flanking the Blacksmith's Hill was a high causeway with steps leading down to a row of cottages, all on different levels, and an area called The Corner. Ted told me that the first of these cottages had been their Scout Hut before the First World War. I was asked to imagine this area as it used to be although it still looks very lovely. It is on the corner of the Banbury Road and it used to have a well kept green with a beautiful chestnut tree in the centre. It was one of the trees from which Ted and his peers used to gather the conkers for the autumn conker games.

Ted pointed to the left of this area where there is a bank, apparently this used to be higher than it is now and was topped by elm trees, this was always called The Hill Trees. We peered in amongst the roots which still exist and were able, with a degree of imagination, to see traces of the fortified wall which used to surround the village.

At the back of this mound there are houses and the whole area is called The Hill, the other side of which is the Hollow Road along which we walked. I was shown where another oil lamp used to illuminate the path. The Hollow Road has high flanking walls on both sides, my question as to the origin of the name received the answer that it was once believed that there had been a watercourse along there but that no one seemed to have remembered anything more than ordinary rain water. The road rises sharply to the Square, the main shopping area of the village. Just before we entered the Square I was shown a really old, Tudor cottage with an outside staircase. In the early days of this century the room at the top of these stairs was used as a storage place for salt. Of course, it was called The Salt House and its large oblong shaped blocks of salt were much in demand at 'pig killing time'. The salt was used for curing the hams and bacon. Most villagers kept a pig, some kept two, and pig meat was the staple meat for the cottagers. Thrifty housewives rendered down the fat to make lard, 'Many's the slice of bread I've eaten spread with lard flavoured with rosemary' said Ted. I confess to a shudder, lard looks so VERY unappetising to me. I have a lovely rosemary bush in my garden which was an early present from Ted and we have noticed that he never passes it without rubbing his hands on it; I wonder if it makes him remember the lard of his childhood?

A few yards further on I was shown the site of still another oil lamp and was told that Aynho had been well illuminated, they had a total of six oil lamps in the village which were lit each night and cared for by the sexton. There was also another Tudor cottage with outside staircase of stone. In the old days this had been a posting inn but that was before the time of my guide. We passed a clock makers, but I was asked to imagine this as it had been, a butcher's shop. Next to it had been the abbattoir, apparently a gruesome but compulsive place to the youth of the village, that is, until the school master asked that it be used only during school hours.

We walked on out of the Square to a green in the centre of which had stood a cross of stone. For many years the base of this cross had stood in the stable yard at Park House where it was used as a mounting block. It was believed that the early cross was the place from which itinerant monks preached before the church was built, but the old cross is no more, instead there stands the sign of the Cartwright Arms Inn.

On past the Cartwright Arms we walked until we reached a row of cottages and then, standing in its own grounds was the Grammar House. This is a very attractive building of old stone, originally, in early Tudor times it was two houses, but in 1654 the two were combined to be used as a Grammar

School. 'Of course,' said Ted, 'this was no longer used in my childhood, it stopped being a school in 1893, it's where the doctor lived.' I asked Ted if he had been to the surgery very often but he thought not although he remembered that the actual surgery was housed in one of the outbuildings which in later years became the estate office. In 1913, the house became the residence of Sir Fairfax and Lady Cartwright. The name was then changed to Grammar House. For a long time it was the last house in the village, Ted told me of taking flowers there for Lady Cartwright, it was obvious that he loved the house and I do not blame him, it is extremely attractive. Opposite the Grammar House I saw modern luxury homes but Ted didn't see them. He saw a big shed and the outbuildings and stables belonging to the Grammar House. These were all destroyed by a huge fire, it was ironic that some of the buildings had once housed the old manual fire engine and, nearby, the headquarters of the Fire Brigade.

There was an entrance to the Church but we did not go into the Church at this time, we walked on down the road to a sharp bend. In the early days of Ted's life this was known as Drovers' Corner, a name it had had for many, many years but then, in 1924 it became known as Wembley Corner because, instead of drovers driving sheep and cattle from the Welsh Hills, there were charabancs (as motor coaches were called in those days) taking people to the Wembley Exhibition from the Midlands and the North of England.

We walked on along the road past Wembley Corner passing the entrance of a house called Friars Well, I asked Ted if this was something to do with the Hostel of bygone days. 'Seems likely' he said but he admitted that he didn't really know. However, he did know that at the beginning of the century it had been the home of the estate agent, he told me that there used to be a marvellous old relic of the past in the grounds of this house. It was a stone built dovecote, the walls eighteen inches thick. It had brick gables which protruded every square foot to provide a resting place for the doves. It had been badly neglected so, in 1955, the decision was made that it must come down. 'Such a loss,' said Ted, 'those old dovecotes have almost all disappeared, if only people would preserve these things then our children's children could enjoy them.' That was rather the theme of much of the comment I heard on that walkabout! But Ted was full of praise for many of the new owners of the cottages, they had tried very hard to maintain the external appearance and so retain the character of the village.

We got back to the car and took the turning beyond Friars Well toward the old station. A mile and a half up this road lies the village of Clifton with its old mill half of which is in Oxfordshire and half in Northamptonshire. All this used to be part of the Aynho estate. A little way down this road is the Oxford Canal (always called The Cut by the old village people), Ted waxed eloquent. 'I can remember the horsedrawn barges bringing tons of coal from the collieries in the Midlands. Our coal was brought there and many a hundred-weight have I wheelbarrowed up the hill to Aynho. And then there were the barge people, they had gaily coloured buckets and bowls on board, I think it was rather like the gypsies and their china, the bargees liked their painted tinware.'

We looked at the old station – 'Aynho for Deddington' – this used to be a regular stopping place for the old Great Western trains and the Great Western Hotel stood there for many a year. Indeed, it still does but not quite in its former glory. Behind the station are the remains of the old clay and gravel pits and the buildings in which bricks were made for the estate.

I was told of the old sale yard which used to be alongside the railway line. The pens were of wood and, again, this was Cartwright property. 'When I was a small boy,' said Ted, this sale yard was swept away to make way for a new branch railway to go to London via Bicester and Princes Risborough, a much shorter and prettier route to London than via Oxford.

Aynho junction begins at Nell Bridge which, at the time of the building of the junction, was still Cartwright property. The story Ted told me was that the Old Squire, William

Cornwallis Cartwright actually gave the land for the junction on condition that should he, or any member of his family, or friends visiting Aynho House be travelling on this fast route they should be able to make a request for the train to stop at Aynho station.

We leaned on a wall and Ted told me of the building of the high viaduct and the tunnel. The viaduct carried the line over the gravel pits, the tunnel was one mile long. These were completed in 1910 and Ted insisted he remembered much of the excitement caused by these buildings.

'The old sale yards were replaced by new ones' said Ted, 'a posh house with catering facilities was built on the Aynho side of the line, the hurdles for the sheep were made from willows growing on the estate and after each sale these hurdles had to be scrubbed and cleaned ready for the next sale in a fortnight, not a very pleasant job.' I asked why the sale yard was no longer active and was told that everything was transferred to Banbury market. 'Many's the penny I've earned driving sheep to Banbury market,' said Ted and he pointed out to me the little house which is all that is left of the sale yard, it looked rather lonely standing there in the middle of a field.

We went back up the hill, passing a road to the right which, I was told, led along the edge of the Park to Souldern Mill, another old mill on the Aynho estate and which, like the one at Clifton, was still in use in the early part of the century. 'Cottagers used to take their grain to one or other of these mills for grinding' said Ted.

Going back to the village we drove past the stocks, these are on the side of the road and I had to confess that I had driven along that road many, many times and had not realised what was behind the little iron fence. These stocks had been erected on the orders of Thomas Cartwright in the early 1700s and had continued in use for over one hundred years. Ted told me that in the Park House was a room known as 'The Justice Room', it was here that the Squire would hear cases against the local miscreants. In early days the Squire had immense powers over the people in the parish.

We went through to the Bicester Road past the allotments, 'These were a feature of the village life' said Ted, 'there were these on the Bicester Road which we called Stan'ell Pits, then there were some others – one called Walton Grounds and the others were Poor's Piece, so called because they were for the very poor and no rent was charged. I don't know how these were allocated, I expect it was done by the Parish Relief people. My father was able, with our garden and his allotment to keep our family in all its vegetable needs.'

On we went out of the village, we passed the entrance to a wood, 'Pest House Wood' said Ted. 'What a horrid name' said I. 'Yes,' said Ted, 'but for a good cause. In the old days, any villager contracting an infectious disease was expelled to an old stone house in this wood, the idea was to prevent the spread of the disease by isolating the victims. I expect a lot never came out of the place. When I was a boy the house had fallen into ruins but its sinister past didn't prevent us using it as a playground. One of the very old gardeners at Aynho Park House once told me that, as a child, he had lived with his parents in the Pest House whilst waiting for a cottage, they were glad to get out!' Ted went on to tell me that the building became dangerous and was demolished in 1924, another piece of history lost! However much of the stone was used for building the Village Hall.

We drove on past a sharp right hand turn going to the village of Croughton but we took the left to the Charlton Road. 'Now,' said Ted 'here's an interesting name, that's Cut Throat Spinney. A man was found there with his throat cut, it is just a story to me, I don't know when it happened or if he was a suicide or a murder case, but I do know that, when I was a boy, a man hanged himself from one of the trees there. Both these men are buried in the churchyard – I'll show you where later. After this second tragedy many of the trees and much of the undergrowth were cleared away.'

A little further along this same Charlton Road we came to Camp Farm. I asked Ted why 'Camp Farm'? 'Well, over in the corner there is an old Roman encampment inside a

170

circular mound topped with trees, so the name is very appropriate!' I asked where the trees were and was told another sad story of the rape of the countryside. It seems the farm and land had been part of the Aynho Estate and when they were sold there was a condition of sale that the trees should remain as they were. 'My brother was involved in the sale' said Ted 'he said the same condition was imposed on the sale of The Butts' trees but both lots were cut down, it was criminal!' 'Yes, Ted, there is something to be said for our modern planning restrictions and regulations. Why is it that a youngster damaging a tree is a vandal, but when grown businessmen rape the countryside by cutting down trees, ploughing up historic sites or grubbing out hedgerows, they are astute business men?'

We drove back and again parked the car in Blacksmith's Hill. We walked up a steep little alley, Skittle Alley. 'I always imagined people in olden dress playing skittles in this alley,' said Ted, 'Can't you imagine them in their ruffs and doublets?' I could, the high stone walls of this narrow way must have seen some interesting sights. On the left Ted pointed to a house where the Secull family had lived, this was the family who had suffered the loss of a daughter but Ted also told me of 'Old Eli Secull' who fell off a roof and broke his foot badly but he wouldn't go to the hospital or anything like that, he let the foot set itself – badly – and, for the rest of his life was on crutches. This opened up an interesting train of thought, 'Tell me, Ted, did the villagers have fear of doctors and hospitals?' 'Our village doctor was well liked and respected, so was the village nurse, but the hospital, well, that was another story.' Ted refused to be drawn on the subject of the hospital so I was left with only stories I had heard in my own youth. Although nearly a couple of decades younger than Ted I remember that my mother would do anything to avoid going to our local hospital. Ted then told me an amusing tale of a small boy who had a boil. His mother took him to the nurse who said it must be lanced by the doctor and that she would take him. The small boy (who spent much of his time in the fields with the farm labourers) stood very still whilst the little operation took place. When it was done he fixed the doctor with a steely look and said 'Come on nurse, we're going to the policeman to have this bugger locked up for hurting me!'

Skittle Alley turned sharply right and there was a delightful house. 'That is where Mrs Czeppe lives, she was village school mistress for many years and was a great friend of my wife, and me' said Ted. 'She came to Aynho in 1930 and was then Miss Govier.'

We walked across the road to Aynho Park House. Ted had 'phoned to ask permission to visit the grounds and so, with the best possible guide, I saw these historic gardens. We walked through the lovely Lime Walk, looked at the entrance to the ice-house, I saw the lovely maidenhair tree, and the platform from which the clay pigeons had been fired. We walked through the Yew Walk, we looked at the pit which Ted had always wanted to use for a lake, we stood on the edge of the ha-ha and looked out over the fields which were once the Park. I closed my eyes and listened to Ted's description. I saw the fair at the Flower Show, with its lighted flares on the stalls, the roundabouts and swings. I saw the peaceful scene with the cattle and deer browsing under the walnut tree and I saw the hustle and bustle of a World War Two Army camp. Sadly, with a nostalgic backward glance we made our way to the Church. Approaching it from this side it was truly a revelation. It looked, not like a church but rather like a country house of the same style as the Park House. We went inside, 'This Church filled a large part of my young life' said Ted. 'Here I was baptised and confirmed, this is the little gap I sat in to pump the organ, that is the pew where the Old Squire always sat, it was funny, he never did stay for the sermon.' 'Perhaps the Rector sent him an advance copy, Ted.' 'He might have done, but somehow I doubt it,' answered my friend.

We continued to look around the Church, there was much of interest and I was loath to leave. I thought of the

Roundheads despoiling the old church, of the Royalists holding services there, of the countless numbers of humble villagers who worshipped there and whose pennies had helped its upkeep. I thought too, of the Cartwright family who had been its patrons for over three hundred years and whose benevolent paternalism had benefitted the village. I thought too, of other villages where squires of a different type made the lives of all their tenants a misery, I remembered some of the stories I had heard in my native Dorset of men who held the lives of their villagers so lightly. We looked up at the tower, 'Those bells have rung in many a New Year' I said to Ted. 'Yes, they used to muffle the bells for some peels before midnight but then, at midnight, the muffles would be taken off and the bells would burst forth in a glorious peel to bring in the New Year.'

We walked round the churchyard. We looked at the gravestones. 'Here lie my father and mother, my sister is named on the stone but she isn't actually buried there but my mother said that my sister should be remembered on the memorial. Here is the grave of Sir Fairfax and Lady Cartwright, and here, with his son by him, lies my old friend and master, Richard Cartwright. I am still sad when I think of him, but have many, many happy memories too. I still bring a wreath of holly to him at Christmas.' Ted pointed out the graves of some of the Roman Catholic members of the family and household and we fell to wondering if, perhaps, the wrought iron head 'stones' were a Catholic, or perhaps an Italian fashion. Lady Cartwright had been of Italian parentage. We looked at the unmarked spot where the two corpses from 'Cut Throat Spinney' had been buried. We walked still more around the graves, 'He was at school with me, she married my cousin, that lady was a great friend of my mother, he was a skilled woodman like my father, he sang in the choir when I was a choirboy, she was a bit of a tartar to her poor old husband, he used to take refuge in the blacksmiths forge,' so said Ted, and I gathered a whole insight into the old village life.

173

Walking back across the front of the house we were stopped by a delightful lady, one of the present residents of the old house. The house was sold to the Mutual Housing Association and is now divided into flats which are bought by retired people, mostly of some standing, the flats aren't cheap! This lady was most interested to hear the identity of my companion and invited us into the house to see, first her own rooms, and then some of the main rooms of the house. This lady had her flat in what had been the butler's quarters. The whole place was a lovely home, she had brought with her many fine pieces of furniture, china and many books. When I showed interest in the books she asked if I would like to see the library, would I just! Having been a librarian for many years (albeit, in industrial rather than public libraries) I have an enormous love of books. There were many, many old volumes, beautifully bound in leather and still in very good condition. I would have liked longer to browse amongst them. The library is a beautiful room and it is easy to imagine it being used by its former owners. I could see the master in embroidered waistcoat and satin breeks, with his powdered wig and his long pipe sitting in a chair reading the paper, or the mistress, in crinoline, reading the latest novels of Mrs Henry Wood. Our guide then took us through the lovely, formal drawing rooms. There are still many pictures and pieces of fine china left by Miss Cartwright, these rooms are still used on special days. The old orangery is now a delightful dining room but again, with Ted's description I could see it a bower of plants and flowers.

We were so very grateful to this kind resident for giving us so much of her time and for inviting us into the house.

We went along to our last port of call, the old greenhouse. The new owner was not at home but we peeped at these buildings which were such a part of my companion's life. I looked at the outside of the bothy and tried to imagine it as the home of a young trainee gardener, sharing with colleagues and being 'cared for' by the wife of another. I thought of Mr and Mrs Brown checking the linen and cleanliness once a month, and poignantly, I thought of it as the first home of this dear old gentleman standing by my side. How proud he must have been of his lovely wife, of course, I did not know her but I've seen pictures of a very attractive lady. Then I giggled, because I had suddenly had a vision of that rather large gentleman, John Humphris, ex Inspector Metropolitan Police, 'planting' his cousin in a rhubarb pot!

We looked in the greenhouses. There were many empty spaces. Some fine tomatoes were growing in one but the other was almost empty. 'Can you imagine this with my Portia flowering? Eight hundred blooms all at once? I shut my eyes, yes, I could see it and marvelled', rather tritely I said 'Big trees from little acorns grow, but this was a big plant from an eight inch pot from Harrods.' Perhaps the most touching thing I saw was the potting bench. There Ted had stood, for nearly sixty years, potting, repotting and making beautiful plants.

Sadly it was time to return home and to the humdrum daily life. But I felt privileged to have been given a glimpse of a way of life completely alien to me. It had taken me about a year to sort and check all the pieces of paper which Ted gave to me. It isn't over yet, we have to go through it together, then it must be typed by someone more expert than I, then, Oh dreaded task! we have to find a publisher because I am sure there must be many, many people who will enjoy to read, as I have done, the reminiscences of a very grand old man.

Index